Divorce is not Destiny

Divorce is not Destiny

by Lynn Kinnaman

Published by Works by Design Publications,
a division of Works by Design, LLC

All scripture verses, unless otherwise indicated, are taken from the New International Version (NIV), The Living Translation (NLT) or The Message Bible (TMB) and are labeled as such.

Lynn@WorksByDesign.com or
PO Box 11083, Bozeman, MT, 59719

To my daughters,
who grew up to be
the best people I know.

Your faith
and your commitment
to the high road
allows
God's light to shine,
even in the darkest places.

Contents

Why I Wrote This Book

The sun was shining and the road stretched ahead of me, full of possibilities and adventure. My dogs napped, my travel trailer followed obediently and I felt a sense of freedom and promise.

It wasn't always that way.

A few years before I'd been in the depths of despair. My 28-year marriage had ended. My husband had moved on and I felt abandoned. There were days I went from the bed to the sofa then back to bed. I'd always been self-motivated, a planner, an achiever. It frightened me that I could no longer picture a desirable future, and my enthusiasm for life simply didn't exist.

I had no hope.

Prior to the divorce, we had declared bankruptcy. It had affected my financial standing much more than his. I had no charge cards, no income and no home. I'd sold my house at a loss and found myself unable to purchase again. I was an emotional wreck.

I couldn't stay in the small town where we lived; I couldn't face another hostile or sympathetic stare. I didn't want to answer any questions or be part of any conversations.

I hurt so much I didn't think I'd survive.

When I hooked the U-Haul to my Subaru during a January snowstorm, my eye twitched uncontrollably and my body vibrated like a tuning fork. I was headed to Arizona, where my aunt, uncle, cousin and his wife lived. My aunt was very ill, but she was anticipating my arrival with delight. She promised a big hug and I knew I'd feel welcome. My cousin and his wife were gracious enough to let me stay with them until I got settled.

My aunt died days before I arrived.

I was mourning everything in my life. My marriage was shattered, my daughters were struggling, I'd left the state in which I'd lived for two decades, quit my job and lost my loving aunt. On top of that, my health was suffering.

Maybe you are feeling the way I did.

If you are, I wrote this book for you.

Divorce shatters your life into fragments and it's difficult to find the pieces, let along put them back together, when your eyes are filled with tears. Whether they are tears of sorrow, frustration or anger, I've been there.

Chances are you're feeling like Alice through the rabbit hole. The landmarks that kept you oriented have disappeared, the language you spoke with friends and family is foreign and incomprehensible. No one understands how you're feeling. Some days you don't even relate to your own life.

The future's uncertain, the past is painful and the present is chaos.

The important thing to know is, no matter now horrible things look right now, you will not be in this place forever. Divorce is a life experience, like other life experiences, and you can let it define you or you can use it to emerge better, stronger and healthier than you were before it happened.

This book is filled with wisdom and practical advice I've gathered from experts, put together with my experience and training. It's not theory. I've lived through what you are facing now.

I've spent the years since my divorce discovering what it takes to heal, working through my challenges, then going beyond to equip myself to help others facing divorce or other personal disasters.

I became a Life Coach and DivorceCare facilitator. Driven by a hunger for information, I researched methods for healing, growth and victory over negative experiences. What I learned went into this book.

On my right ring finger, I wear a diamond set in white gold. It's a symbol, a reminder, for me. When I married, we selected a yellow-gold engagement ring and found a unique wedding band that complemented it. After my divorce, I wanted a new beginning for me and for my diamond. I had the help of a long-time friend, who worked in a jewelry store, to encourage me.

My stone had a small chip in it, which had happened during the course of wearing it for nearly three decades. I found a new setting that concealed the flaw and displayed the stone to its best advantage. The resulting ring is a brilliant illustration of renewal.

The design and the significance of the resetting inspired me. I wrote a story about it, called "A Flash of Brilliance", that appeared in *Chicken Soup for the Soul: Divorce and Recovery.*

I believe we can all reset our future, taking a diamond of a life, flaws and all, and reframing it to allow it to shine.

It's a process that begins with healing and never ends, as you discover more about yourself and your possibilities.

Divorce has happened to you, but it is not you.

Divorce is not destiny.

Section One

~Devastation~

Devastate:
To cause someone severe and overwhelming shock or grief, to destroy or ruin

The trip I was taking with my travel trailer and doggies had been carefully planned to accomplish a couple of things. It grew from one of those "poor little me" moments we all have. After a conversation when I'd listened to yet another friend detail exciting travel plans, I'd hung up the phone with mixed feelings.

I was happy for her, but it underscored my solitary existence. I had a great 19-foot RV, but few people around me who could or would go camping. So I was stuck at home. Because I was alone. *Boo-hoo.*

Then the stubborn kid inside me jumped up in protest. *That's stupid*, she said. Not a tactful child, this one. *There's no reason in the world you can't take yourself on a camping trip.*

It wasn't a new thought. When I bought the trailer, I pictured myself taking off at will, traveling to interesting places and meeting new people. I'm always more daring and adventurous in my mind.

In reality, when I get close to fulfilling a desire that stretches me a bit, the negative voices get louder; the doubts grow larger until I chicken out.

Still, the fact that I could imagine a trip was a testament to how far I'd come, because for the first few years after the divorce it was impossible for me to dream. I couldn't muster enthusiasm for another day, or visualize a future.

My trip was designed to prove to myself I could do it, to push out of my comfort zone and accomplish something I'd said I'd wanted but had not tried. To see if I could take a dream and make it a reality. The second purpose was to shake up my creativity. Changing my environment was a proven way to get my imagination out of a rut, and I welcomed the jolt.

Ambition had returned. After a long dry spell, ideas were emerging and possibilities were swirling around me like snowflakes. I was ready to take action.

Right now you may feel like you'll never be able to reach for the stars again. You might think that when you get up in the morning, you've maxed out your potential for the day. This baffles you, because you don't understand why you can't pull yourself together, the way you have in every crisis you've faced in the past.

If you look at your divorce in the same way as a physical injury, it helps put it in perspective.

If you'd been in a car accident, broken your leg, sustained bruises and sprains, you wouldn't expect to be back to normal in a day, a week, or even a month. Friends wouldn't advise you to "snap out of it" or "just get over it" because it would be obvious that you had serious healing to do. You had major damage to your body.

Divorce is major damage to your heart and soul. It, too, requires serious healing.

Yet we are so impatient in a situation like this, where the destruction is internal and not marked by a visible scar. We expect to be able to "buck up" and get through it simply because we want to. That belief is reinforced when others expect the same. However, it's not going to happen like that, and here's why.

You are grieving. Whether the marriage was good or difficult, when you got married you had dreams and hopes. You were in love. You had a vision of what your future would be like with this other person. Maybe it was like that for a time, perhaps a long time. But now the marriage has ended, and so have those dreams.

Acknowledge the loss, don't try to sweep it away in an effort to be stoic. Respect your pain. In the same way that physical pain keeps you from pushing a broken body, emotional pain is a big stop sign, and if you ignore it, you'll compound the damage.

The sorrow you feel is in proportion to the depth of your love and your belief that this relationship was going to be everything you'd imagined. If you hadn't cared so much about it, you wouldn't be hurting now.

The death of a dream, the end of your hopes for the life you'd envisioned, is not a trivial event. It's not something you can put away and leave behind without tremendous agony. If you try to rush yourself, it's the same as if you try to walk on a broken leg. It's foolish. You might double or triple the time needed for healing.

Here's a scary thought. You could even make it impossible for your leg, or your life, to ever return to its healthy, complete state.

Which leaves the path that's necessary, but one none of us wants to walk. The path of healing. It requires paying attention to your injuries, feeling those feelings, respecting your limitations and enduring the process as it is. This is a traumatic passage.

It's gonna hurt.

You'll feel intense emotion and overwhelming sorrow.

Someone might tell you divorce is so common today, so many people get divorced, it's no big deal. Implying that for you to take time to grieve makes you abnormal, selfish or weak. It's true that divorce is common, with nearly 50% of marriages ending in that way, but it doesn't mean your experience is trivial or easy.

You go to sleep thinking about the divorce. When you wake

up, it's still on your mind. Your life feels like an endless crisis. Your emotions might frighten you because you can't control them. You might act in ways that surprise you, and even try to disappear in alcohol, drugs or new relationships.

Anything to escape the pain.

It's understandable. No one wants to hurt, but there are no shortcuts to healing, only temporary fixes that leave bigger problems when they wear off.

I lived in a small, small town, with a population of less than 2000 residents. If you don't know what it's like, I'm sure you can imagine. It felt as if our personal business was everybody's business. We moved there when my husband was well-established in his affair and I'd innocently transplanted myself into enemy territory.

His friends, her friends and no friends for me.

With Labor Day weekend coming up, I prepared for work and thought about how things had deteriorated between us. That Friday morning I couldn't ignore my fears anymore. I confronted him. After a civil (on his part) and emotional (on mine) discussion, where he admitted the affair had been going on for years, we agreed to divorce. On my way out the door to go to my job, he asked if we were still going camping with family and friends for the weekend.

I froze, scenarios running through my head.

It's funny. There are situations that, if you heard about them, you'd swear you'd never tolerate. Clear as black and white. You would not be put in that position. Then life turns a corner and you're faced with something so bizarre and surreal you take a step back. When you consider your choices, you realize you've just entered uncharted territory. With no map to guide you, no rules to follow, you have to make a choice. It didn't feel like much of a choice. As I weighed my sorry options, little did I know this would not be the last time I'd be forced to choose between the insane and the absurd. Things were only going to get crazier.

Blessedly, the Lord unfolds our days without allowing us to see all that's coming. And that's how we have to approach it, each moment as a step. One foot in front of the other.

So I considered. I thought about how horrible it would be to go camping. Then I thought about staying home, alone, while my family and friends were out of town and far away. I pictured myself, forsaken, in my empty home. I thought of how everyone would go on without me, enjoying a tradition that had been a part of my summers for the past 10 years.

Ultimately, it was a no-brainer. I had to be with my family, even if it would be awkward and painful.

We went camping.

When we returned, he retrieved a few things from the house. He was taking the trailer to live in while he sorted things out. As we stood on the driveway, I looked at the man I had fallen in love with as a 16-year-old and had loved for decades. We'd been through so much, but at this point what I saw in his eyes was a desire to get away.

"Well," he said. "Have a good life."

"You, too," I replied. And he was gone.

My devastation felt overwhelming, but then, one week later, our country experienced a horrific attack and the world itself turned upside down. It was the 11th of September, and as I watched the disaster replay on television over and over, the loss and destruction echoed my own personal tragedy. I felt empty and desolate.

Getting through each day became a massive challenge. Doing anything, simply thinking of doing anything, exhausted me.

At first I had to set tiny goals. Get up in the morning. Brush my teeth, fix my hair. I worked on auto-pilot. My despair festered like a blemish on my face – I was hyper-aware of it. Certain that it was visible to everyone. It became an obstacle that affected every interaction. Normal chores loomed, as impossible to tackle as scaling Mt. Everest. Doing laundry was monumental. Bill-paying was an event in itself. It was all I could do for that day. It took everything out of me.

I wanted it to go away. I wanted to curl up in the corner of my room and stay there. Opt-out of living and settle for existing.

Our first grandchild was born a month later. What should have been a time of joy was tainted by the need to schedule visiting times separately, to take turns. I felt so cheated. Babies were a celebration, a joy I should be sharing with my husband.

Our daughter had married a great guy and they'd produced a miracle. Yet I didn't get to be the proud grandmother, I was the heartbroken ex-wife. I was the obstacle, the difficult one. I couldn't stand the idea of sharing my children, and now my grandchildren, with an outsider.

After the baby came, I wanted to be there for my daughter as she experienced first-time motherhood. While that was my desire, I didn't have anything left inside. I didn't know how to care for myself emotionally, and had nothing available to offer my beloved children. My younger daughter graduated and came home after spending 3 ½ years a thousand miles away. She came home to disaster. A mother who was barely keeping herself together.

Newton's law worked for a while. *A body in motion tends to stay in motion unless acted on by an outside force.* Keep moving forward. I did it by rote.

Then the outside force fell with the weight of a two-ton boulder. It wasn't that the incident was so huge, it was the cumulative effect of little incidents nipping at me, drawing blood and draining my energy.

A woman at work was talking about a party she'd attended, describing my husband's behavior in colorful and vivid language. He was the good-time guy. The party guy. I couldn't believe what I was hearing. Didn't she wonder where his wife had been? I was becoming invisible, dispensable. I felt myself shrinking into oblivion, unnoticed by everyone.

I couldn't let myself disappear.

It was January. On my break at work I went outside to the loading dock with my cell phone. I was crying. I called my mother in California, telling her I could not remain a moment more. Could I come stay with her for a while?

No.

My mother had problems of her own. I needed another plan.

I was determined. Reverting to sheer animal desperation, getting out became my sole focus. It meant leaving my daughters, but I had to go. I had to get away from the people, the situation, the conversations. I had to go away so I could regroup and put myself back together in private.

I called my cousin and his wife, who lived in Arizona. My aunt and uncle lived there, too. Precious family connections. Even though it had been a while, they responded with love and invited me to stay with them. My aunt was ill but anxious to see me. I looked forward to it, but sadly she died just before I got there. My arrival blended my sorrows with those of my cousins and uncle and we mourned together.

They gave me a place to live, a room in their house. But they gave me much more. They loved me. They didn't try to fix me, they didn't lecture me. They listened and they let me deal with it at my own pace.

I'd grown up in the church. I knew I needed to reconnect with that solid rock of faith. God guided me to a Christian women's book group. I made some tentative connections and found myself sobbing again. Their response was a salve to my broken heart. They were concerned and sympathetic. They cared.

I decided to meet with the pastor. Here again, God was gracious to me. The pastor wasn't thinking of himself when I came to his office. He wasn't worried about lawsuits or propriety. He didn't prop the door open or ask his secretary to sit in. He was focused on the devastated human being in need that God had brought him, and God knew that anything less would have sent me running from the church.

The pastor listened. After I told my story, he said, "That sucks, doesn't it."

Those words, which some might condemn as ungodly or disgusting, were exactly what I needed to hear. God in his wisdom brought me to a person who, with four little words of genuine empathy, demonstrated he understood my suffering and heard my cry. He wasn't going to bury me in homilies or lectures. He was willing to let me talk, and he responded with compassion. That human reaction showed me the pastor cared for the state of my soul and the depth of my sorrow. He wasn't trying to stifle me, avoid me or dismiss my story. He listened. Intently. He felt my pain. When we prayed, I felt, by extension, that God ached for me, too.

I started attending church regularly and as time went by, I got re-baptized to declare my new commitment to God and his ways.

But I was far from healed.

Section Two
~Triage~

Triage:
Assessing and assigning priority, usually in emergency situations, according to degrees of urgency

The divorce was proceeding and I needed a place to live. I found an apartment complex that would allow dogs, but I couldn't rent it by myself because of our previous financial difficulties and the fact I was a single, unemployed woman.

I had to ask my daughter and her husband to co-sign so I could get approved. It was humbling to have to beg favors. On the other hand, it was thrilling to be able to have personal space. I moved into a small second-story apartment overlooking an arroyo. I didn't have much furniture, I'd left most of it in Montana. My cousins gave me a bed and I had a papasan chair in the living room, a table and chairs I'd gotten at Kmart and my television and computer from home. Plus one of my dogs.

I'd never lived by myself. It was alien and wonderful, as were the scorpions and Javelinas that shared the environs.

A brave new world.
The divorce process was a sliver of the event the wedding

had been. Strange that an entire lifetime, my whole adult existence, came down to a few minutes of long-distance court time. I stood on the balcony, on the phone to Bozeman, as the judge pronounced us divorced.

The finality of the declaration shook me. I'd passed the point of no return. He wasn't going to have last-minute regrets and ask to try again. It was over. I was no longer a wife. I was a divorcee, an ugly word in my ears. Unwanted. Discarded.

However, God gave me a feisty temperament. I was down, for sure, but refused to be counted as out. I forced myself forward, trying to formulate the next step.

I needed a job.

At the time, I couldn't see God's hand working, guiding me. As I look back today, I see it clearly.

The job I found was working at a non-profit created by a woman who had triumphed over serious physical disabilities. She had an unquenchable spirit, a zest for life and compassion for others. Daily I saw the difference small things made in people's lives. She believed in focusing on one person at a time instead of trying to reach everyone. It was an experience that proved to be invaluable in creating the person I was to become, and while it affected me then, I wouldn't appreciate the full extent of the impact until much later.

It did help balance my attitude. Don't get me wrong, I still had to go through the suffering, hurt and pain but I also was surrounded by people who were accomplishing great things in the lives of others. It inspired me. I'd always been a volunteer and soon found myself working at a homeless shelter in Phoenix. I don't even remember how I got connected with the organization, but I did, and it felt good to know I could contribute, in some small way, to improving someone else's situation.

Getting away and mending myself before I went back home again had been a good idea. I could have used more time, but life has a way of changing the best-laid plans.

My older daughter became pregnant with her second child. After traveling back and forth for the holidays and knowing another baby was on the way, I had to make a tough choice. Arizona had been a haven for me. There were lots of activities and I never had to worry that I'd run into my ex and his girlfriend.

But my precious daughters were in Montana. I could not rebuild relationships from 800-plus miles away.

That tipped the scale. I was moving home.

My mother pitched in financially to help me buy a small manufactured home in Belgrade and I packed up and relocated. My emotions, which had settled a bit in Arizona, were raw again. Returning to Montana ripped the scabs off and the wounds bled anew.

I was reunited with my daughters, but we were light-years away from the relationship we'd once had. I discovered the girlfriend of my ex was pregnant and he was going to marry her. My daughters were going to have a sister. A sister younger than my two grandchildren. It was another one of those through-the-looking-glass moments. I was falling and grasping for something to stop my descent. I searched for a church.

Divorce can be a difficult situation for churches. Often it's not something they are equipped for or eager to handle. Some worry that to acknowledge divorce implies they condone it. There's a fear that if they comfort and support divorced people, they are enabling the act and might even encourage it.

This is tainted thinking that slams the door on thousands of men and women who need God and need to reconnect to God more at this time than any other in their lives. It's been described as "shooting our wounded".

We don't want your problems. We don't know how to deal with you. Go somewhere else.

Even if most churches welcome the emotionally wounded, those that don't stand in the way of seekers connecting with the ultimate Healer. God commands that we love one another. That we don't judge. He forgives, and so should we.

I eventually landed at a small church where they welcomed me. As I see it in retrospect, God found a place where I could settle, then opened my eyes to the shattering need in my community for compassionate support of divorced people. I got a glimpse of the plan he had for me and I was ready to get started.

I discovered the biblically-based program for healing and recovery called DivorceCare, and contacted an experienced facilitator in a distant town who met with me and gave me the benefit of her experience with the program.

With her advice and materials in hand, I approached the church about it. DivorceCare has to have a church under which to function, so their involvement was essential. I got the go-ahead.

I started the first group to span the holiday season, because my experience had been that the holidays were tough. I had an amazing group of attendees. As we worked our way through the 13-week series I was blessed tremendously by the program and the individuals on the journey with me.

I did plenty of research about divorce, recovery and living abundantly in addition to what I learned in DivorceCare, because I wanted to find out everything I could about what we, as divorced people, were facing.

I was driven, because I intended to heal and I knew it wouldn't happen without education and hard work. God nudged me along that path, revealing that my experiences were going to give me something to offer others going through divorce or facing other life-changing challenges.

Hope, fragile but persistent, pushed through the cold snow of my sorrow like a tiny tulip seeking the sun. God had planted the seed and the warmth of his love was coaxing growth from the frozen ground of my despair.

WALKING THE WALK

I discovered there's a pattern to grieving and restoration. One model that's used frequently is the Kübler-Ross Five Stages of Grief.

If you aren't familiar with it, Elizabeth Kübler-Ross wrote a book called *On Death and Dying* in 1969, which described five stages people go through when diagnosed with a terminal illness. This model has been extended to describe stages of grief as it applies to all grieving. Whether it is accurate for all grieving has been a subject of debate, but the stages do help us recognize the normal human reactions to be expected when mourning a loss.

The stages are: Denial, Anger, Bargaining, Depression and Acceptance.

The stages are not linear, and they don't progress as steps. They intertwine, they can be experienced simultaneously, and one might disappear only to reappear later. Identifying the process helps us identify some of the standard emotions we face, and it's a relief to know these stages are normal.

Stage One: Denial

Denial is usually the first reaction to the idea that your relationship has ended. The more invested you were, the harder it is to believe. Like the cartoon where the coyote runs off the cliff and suddenly realizes he's running in mid-air, you can't accept the new reality until you start the downward plunge. Initially, you're in shock. Your thoughts are banging into each other like cars at a demolition derby. You want things to go back to the way they were, get another chance, do things differently.

Having gone through a couple of major traumas, I can tell you to be careful of the decisions you make during this time. We don't recognize shock in ourselves. We keep moving forward through our days, thinking we are making good solid choices. You might feel, as I did, that you are handling things well, being über competent and efficient. Until later, when you discover some of the decisions you made were off-base or even harmful. A trusted friend in whom you can confide and discuss big decisions with will be an important asset.

Denial can take various forms. One of them is to minimize your pain. While that can be appropriate later on, at this stage of the process it's important to allow yourself to grieve without guilt, without condemnation.

One way people try to diminish what they're going through is to compare it to others. Yes, compared to genocide or starvation, divorce is a minor tragedy. However, it's the biggest thing in your life right now. If you have children, it's something that threatens their happiness and way of life. If you scale the impact - one person-one event - you see the devastation is personally significant.

If you downplay your grief, or allow others to, it might feel virtuous but it's unhealthy. A doctor would be negligent if he tried to treat your bruises and broken leg after a cursory examination. Imagine if he said, "Well, we have people with cancer and other deadly diseases here, and you have a broken leg, so we'll put a bandage on it and you can go."

Responsible medical staff would take an X-ray, do a thorough exam, make sure there isn't additional damage that's not visible. They'd ask your history so they could prescribe the right medication, they'd treat your broken leg like the most important problem facing them at that particular moment.

Your divorce, and the changes it brings, is *your* most important problem at the moment.

You can't heal until you recognize the depth of the injury. You can't get better if you say, "It's not cancer, so it's not important," and try to hobble out of the emergency room.

There is a difference between grieving and wallowing. Wallowing is when you get mired in the process of grieving, self-pity and misery well past any reasonable time frame for recovery. It's something to be aware of much farther down the road, not when you're first trying to cope.

There will be a time to move out of grief. There will be a time you will pull yourself up from the misery you've felt and put your life together again. At that time you can do what we all do eventually – compare your situation to others and acknowledge there are other life-altering events that are equal to or worse than divorce.

But that time is not now.

Right now, in this moment, your world has imploded. Right now, during this stage, it is about you.

When you're in an airplane, the emergency drill reminds parents to put on their air mask before they try to help their child. The reason is simple. An unconscious parent is no help to anyone. Someone who doesn't take care of herself becomes part of the problem, not part of the solution.

It's not indulgence; it's responsible to care for yourself. Others may not know what to do, how to help. You might be the only one looking out for you.

Begin by honoring your feelings, not dismissing them. This might feel strange. Maybe you were brought up to think your feelings aren't important or that you can't trust them. To compound that, right now your emotions don't feel trustworthy. They are alien, unfamiliar, monumental or unpredictable.

I know the early days for me were like a roller-coaster of highs and lows. I was ambushed by grief. I'd be having a normal day, even feeling a little smug because I had things under control, I was functioning. Then, with no warning, I'd hear a song or a comment, or have a thought that would puncture my tenuous composure and I'd crumble.

I can remember, right after we had agreed to divorce but before I left Montana, I would fall apart at work. I used to go in the closet and cry. I didn't want people to see me and I couldn't control myself. It seems it's always at that exact moment people decide they need you to handle a work issue. I'd hear them searching for me and I knew I couldn't hide forever. I'd emerge mopping my face, stopping in the bathroom where I'd splash cold water and try to get back to normal. I'm not a pretty weeper and my puffy face made no secret that I was suffering.

It frustrated me to have such little control over my emotions. I didn't know then that it was normal, it was okay. I felt crazy, trapped, frantic. With the exception of a few who had experienced divorce first-hand, people either ignored me or suggested I toughen up.

If grieving your marriage is normal, why do so many people, especially friends and family, push so hard, so soon, for you to get past it?

I didn’t understand then, but I do now. Usually it’s because they love you and don't want to see you suffer. Your pain makes them uncomfortable, it’s awkward being around you, and they don’t know what to say. They don't know what to do to relieve your heartache, so they want you to get better.

Now.

Fix it. Snap out of it. Be yourself again.

You will be yourself again, but it’s not going to happen on someone else’s schedule.

The time line for recovery can vary from situation to situation, and from person to person. The rule of thumb, determined by the experts, is approximately one year of recovery required for every four years married. When I first heard that, my heart sank. I would be an old lady by the time my seven years had passed. Was there any way I could speed it up?

I wanted to skip over the painful parts and get to the good stuff. Being whole again.

However, the process itself contributes to the quality of your future life. Here's an example of what that means. I found an article about a study in London which illustrates the importance of following each step. In this study, researchers analyzed the development stages of 15,000 babies.

Babies who didn't crawl were more likely to be behind in cognitive development and have behavioral problems at the age of five. Crawling, it seemed, taught the baby where their bodies were in relation to other objects, and built strength and coordination. Alternating right and left legs and arms, the way you do when you crawl, helps develop both sides of the brain.

Skipping over the crawling stage may seem like advanced development to the uninformed but it could impair progress later in life.

For best results, you have to crawl before you can walk. And walk before you can run. There are no effective shortcuts.

In the first year after my divorce I joined some on-line dating services. I was tired of being asked if I was dating and getting funny looks when I said no. I didn't have much interest in it but everyone seemed to think I should be looking for Mr. Right. That I *deserved* a relationship, implying that by not having a boyfriend I was somehow being short-changed.

I bought into it. It's what we see on TV, read about. Love is in the air, and without a romance, you lack value. You're insignificant without a significant other. A new romance would mean I'd gotten over my divorce, would mean I was desirable. If somebody loved me, it would show the world I still mattered.

It sounded right.

I figured if my life looked normal, conventional, I could fool everyone, including myself.

There was just one little problem. I couldn't pull it off. I couldn't act like I was fine. I wasn't fine. The last thing I needed was a romantic relationship.

In facilitating DivorceCare, I find the no-dating stipulation to be a major obstacle for some people, even though there are numerous reasons not to jump into another relationship until you've healed. If you are still working on getting past your grief, dealing with your anger, finding a path to forgiveness, you won't have time to develop a new relationship. If you stop your process and focus solely on the relationship, it's called arrested development. You'll be stuck in your misery, but using the other person to distract you from feeling and moving forward.

If you're not healed, but instead in the midst of your recovery, how are you going to connect with a healthy person? Angry people, miserable people, bitter people are not at the top of the desirable partner list. Is that the type of person who will have a successful relationship? Is that the type of person you would seek?

How attractive is someone who complains about their ex-spouse endlessly, who plots revenge at every turn? How about someone who drink incessantly, uses sex as a drug, or uses drugs, period? What about someone who expects you to fix everything that's gone wrong in their life? Do you want to be the bandage on their wound?

You may find someone before you are healed, but will it be a person worthy of you or just a stop-gap to make you feel better? Hooking up to boost your self-esteem isn't fair to you or the other person. What if they fall for you, but you continue healing and decide they aren't the one? Or vice-versa? It would be like falling down stairs while you're still on crutches. Ouch.

Result? Longer healing time and more damage.

Sex, drugs and rock 'n roll will distract you, but they won't heal you. To revisit to the car crash analogy, it's as if you stagger from the wreckage, gulp a handful of painkillers and hop on the back of a rodeo bull. It may be a wild ride, but there won't be much left of you at the end. If you survive, it will be a miracle if you're ever completely sound again.

So why do we go for that bull?

If you've been left by your spouse, you feel abandoned. In my case, I also felt rejected and betrayed. When you're married, you're part of a couple. You're invited places as a couple, you entertain as a couple, and you file taxes as a couple. People see you, they ask where your spouse is. You're linked, in God's eyes and in man's. Once uncoupled, you feel lost. To make matters worse, you're treated differently.

When you're divorced, couples hesitate to include you in their plans because you're the third wheel. One spouse may be threatened by your availability and fear that you might be interested in their partner. If they do include you, you might be in for a rough time.

This happened to me when I was still new in the divorce. I was invited to what I seem to recall as a Valentine's get-together, which, in retrospect, should have been warning enough. However, I knew the women and they assured me I would have a nice time at their couple's party even though I'd be alone.

In their defense, I don't think they really understood how horrible they were that night. Conversation revolved around how each couple met, with charming little stories about courtship and marriage. They stood around in the kitchen, nuzzling each other and whispering together.

I was fresh from my split, raw with rejection and loneliness. I became uncomfortable and, frankly, a little angry. I wanted to leave.

"Well," said one woman whom I had considered a friend. "You really need to get over it." She cuddled her husband possessively.

Easy for you to say, I thought.

I knew I couldn't withdraw from society completely. I needed people. I just needed the right people. In the same way a broken leg requires a cast and crutches to help it heal properly, I had to construct a framework around my broken heart. I wouldn't have to keep that level of protection in place forever, but without it recovery would be difficult.

This meant I had to take a hard look at those around me. There are people and situations I can tolerate now that would have crushed me back then. I can run with the best of them today because my emotional legs are strong. They will take me where I want to go, but when I was first divorced, those legs were broken and weak. It would have been madness for me to try to run in that condition.

Exposing yourself to hurtful, cruel or insensitive people when you are most vulnerable is equally crazy. You can't wrap yourself in cotton but you can use common sense. Your cast and crutches, your framework for healing, should include the right people and positive situations.

Eliminate toxic people. It might seem harsh, but they will cause you more distress by being present than they ever will in their absence. Clearing out the negative influences makes room for new friendships that support your recovery.

There are people around who uplift you, but you need to seek them out. Look for and find friends who are good for you. Not party people, not sexual partners, but friends who will help you get better. At this stage of your recovery, it's most helpful if they are of your same gender. That means women find women friends, men find men friends.

They don't have to be single too, although that can make it easier because they'll probably have flexibility in their lives and be more available. The important part is that they are healthy and caring. When I returned to Bozeman, I floundered for a while, then began to connect with women who were positive, who were believers and who accepted me, warts and all.

The acceptance piece is crucial. If you've been through divorce, you don't want to surround yourself with people bent on "fixing" and "improving" you. There is time for outside help, if you feel you need it, later. Right now you want people in your life who let you be you and afford the space to move through your recovery at the speed that's appropriate.

A divorce group can be helpful, or a coach, counselor or pastor who is familiar with divorce recovery. Understand that those who have no personal experience with divorce are often not aware of the depth of pain or the healing process. Book learning isn't always adequate. The same people who would never tell a widow or widower to snap out of it might tell a divorced person to stop being so self-absorbed and just get on with their life. The curious thing is, they might believe this is helpful advice.

If you're bewildered and susceptible, this will plunge you back into the cycle of trying to deny or skip over your feelings before you've dealt with them.

Be patient with yourself, and at this super-vulnerable time, take care to surround yourself with those who do understand and won't rush you.

Stage Two: Anger

My daughters and I had always been close, but the divorce tested the strength of our bonds. I wanted them to hate him for what he'd done, for leaving me, but we'd raised them too well, it seemed. Being adults, they were able to express the feelings shared, but not always said, by children of divorce.

"He's our father," they'd say. "We love both of you."

My head understood but my heart broke. I was an only child. My daughters and my spouse were my family, the fulfillment of a longing I'd had my entire life. Now I'd lost them.

I wanted someone on my side. I wanted someone to hug me and tell me it was a rotten deal, and I had every right to be devastated. I wanted someone to understand I was destroyed. When no one did, I felt along, rejected, forsaken. I got angry.

Anger is the second stage in the classic grief model.

Anger was huge for me.

It's easier to be angry than to hurt. Anger feels like progress. It gives you something proactive to do. It's energizing and consumes your thoughts. Being angry felt much better to me than feeling wretched.

It also distracted me from experiencing my pain, and it enabled my denial. I welcomed it with open arms. I was interesting to be around in those days, catapulting from miserable to furious, defeated to confrontational. Anger produced adrenaline. Adrenaline made me feel alive.

It was a great improvement over feeling dead, which was the way I had been feeling. For a while anger, and the hormone it released, was my drug of choice.

My anger also came from fear. I was terrified. I was alone, with no allies. The man I had counted on to stay by my side had abandoned me. Who could I trust now? It would be easy to take advantage of me, to squash me, to rob me of my possessions and my emotional stability.

Anger helped me take the offensive. It made me feel stronger. *They won't mess with me if they think I'll make a scene.* Like a dog with bared teeth and a nasty growl, I held the crowd at bay. *Back off,* my anger said, *stay away. I don't want you to hurt me and I can't trust you to be fair.*

Anger does that for us, which is why it works, in a bubble-gum and duct tape sort of way. While it may hold things together for a while, sooner or later it will fail you. The wheels will come off, and you'll crash.

I knew I had to find a way through it because it was costing me. Forgiveness was a key component, which we will discuss in detail later, but for now, let's focus on whether there is any value in the anger.

From a spiritual standpoint, the experts tell us, anger itself is not a sin; it's what you do with it that can be sinful. Righteous anger can inspire action that solves problems, locally and globally. However, most of us are dealing with personal anger that feels righteous to us. This type of anger, when allowed to run rampant, can lead to bad choices and destruction. Anger is one of the biggest causes of stress and persistent stress can be deadly. It raises your adrenaline and your cortisone levels. It increases your heart rate and your blood pressure. Sustained anger is hard on your body.

It's been known for a long time that repressed anger isn't beneficial. The question becomes, if you don't suppress it, what do you do with it? Years ago, the school of thought was that people should physically act out their anger. Therapist offices had foam bats, pillows and other props people would use to bash each other. The theory was this would release the anger and let it dissipate harmlessly. The reality was different. By acting out, people grew more angry, not less.

The same thing happens when you churn your anger endlessly. If it becomes your major topic of conversation, it's passed the helpful venting stage and entered the "I've created a monster" stage. The more you talk about how angry you are, the more it grows. It's magnified and expanded until everything you do and say is affected. You have to break the cycle.

There is a beautiful Native American legend, attributed to the Cherokee nation, which explains it well, and I paraphrase it here.

A grandfather is teaching his grandson about life, and he explains that there are two wolves inside him, fighting. One is evil; full of jealousy, hatred, anger, greed, resentment and lies. The other is good; full of joy, love, compassion, acceptance, forgiveness and peace.

The boy is transfixed, imagining the terrible fight going on within his grandfather. "Which one will win?" he asks.

The grandfather looks at his grandson. "The one that wins," he says, "is the one I feed."

Which wolf are you feeding?

If you don't want anger to take over your life, you must stop nurturing it.

Advice about dealing with anger comes down to two things: 1) Don't stuff it, and 2) Don't escalate it.

Examine the anger. Where is it coming from? Is it from being wronged? Is it because things didn't go the way they should? Is it from disappointment? Like all the emotions you're feeling, the anger has a source, and it is worthwhile to respect your reaction and examine it.

The next question is; is it something you can change? If you've been treated badly and it's a situation you can modify, try that. For example, if someone trampled your feelings by acting in a certain way, and it made you angry, think about what you can do so it doesn't happen again. Rehearse how you can explain to them, without assigning blame, that the way they handled things was not helpful. Ask them if they'd do it differently next time. Then let it go. You've expressed your feelings politely, asked for change and now it's out of your hands.

Let's look at another scenario. You might be angry because you can't mow your lawn. Your spouse took the lawn mower and you can't afford to buy a new one. It's not fair and it's frustrating. It makes you angry, and triggers your emotions about all the things related to the divorce.

Okay, acknowledge that. Then try searching for solutions. It might be possible to join forces with your neighbors. One enterprising young person, one lawn mower and five lawns can add up to a win all the way around. The young person earns extra summer spending money and lawns are done with a small investment. This is a simple example, but sometimes there's a simple solution, only you can't see it because you are so angry.

The lawn is a good example because it was a problem for me. I had never mowed a lawn. I didn't own a mower. I borrowed one from a friend and tackled the front yard. I'm allergic to grass. My shoes turned green, but I got it done.

The backyard needed mowing, too. I didn't want to do it, had no money to hire it done and rebelled. Against myself, as it turned out. I let the stuff back there grow, and grow, and grow. My dogs could get lost in my postage-stamp sized yard. I began to worry that there was some ordinance against such tall weeds and I might be fined. So I finally got out there and tackled it.

It took me weeks. I could only mow about three square feet at a time, and not every day. I eventually made it through, right before fall set in and the snow came.

Possibly you can change the circumstances that provoke the anger. If, for example, the arrangements you have for sharing custody include transferring the children when your spouse's girlfriend or boyfriend is present, which upsets you, see if a different arrangement can be made that would allow for a more peaceful transition.

Practice your reactions. Use your imagination to visualize the situation and find ways to interact without anger. By retraining your response you give yourself an alternative to impulsive actions and increase your control.

Even after you make adjustments, there will still be things you can't change. However, anger won't change them, either, and will hamper your ability to think of alternatives. Anger about a situation that's in the past or is irreversible will eat at you but not be resolved. Like a hamster in a cage, you'll run yourself ragged but never get anywhere. To help manage it, ask yourself a few questions.

What is this anger doing for you? How does it make you feel?

Be honest, and you might discover the anger is driving you to act in ways that harm you and the constant turmoil is giving you headaches, stomach aches or body aches. By listing the effects of your anger, you might realize it's not serving you at all.

Imagine your life without the anger. What would it look like? How would your actions be affected if they were not coming from an angry place? Picture yourself waking up, moving through your day, doing your job, going to bed at night. How would that change if you weren't angry? Most importantly, what would your future look like when not limited by your anger?

Picturing a life without anger might be enough motivation to change.

If it's not, you might still be clinging to anger you believe is justified. We're a stubborn lot, and anger is a life preserver on the tumultuous seas of grief. I know I felt like if I let go I'd sink into the waters of misery. I'd disappear beneath the waves.

Still, I had to admit the anger was making everything in my life worse.

What happened was in the past. I couldn't change it. All the anger in the world would not earn me a do-over. I had to find a way to let it go.

The wrong that was done to you is history. Have you, or anyone you know, ever been able to change the past? Will all the anger in the world alter the fact that it happened? It can't be changed. It's done. Over. Unless you keep the memory of your hurt alive by reliving it. The good news is, now that you know that you don't have any reason to cling to it, your reaction to it can change. Your reality today can change.

Sometimes the door to let go of anger is one of compassion. Understanding, or seeing the whole picture, can redefine your perspective.

One summer our family was camping near the edge of a lake, with a few other RV's around. There was an older trailer with a generator. The generator would run, shut off for a short time, then fire up again. This went on all night, disturbing the serenity of the campground. By morning everyone was plenty annoyed. We approached the campers, and one of the men came over to us, looking contrite.

“I apologize,” he said. “I know the generator is irritating.”

“Yes,” we agreed, ready to elaborate.

“I’m sorry. See, my friend is dying. His wish was to spend the weekend at the lake one last time. The generator keeps his oxygen going. I'm really sorry it's so loud.”

In that instant, anger evaporated like early morning fog. Our perception had been wrong. Learning the truth changed everything. We went back to our own camp, humbled.

It’s not always that clear. Sometimes you won't get the story behind the act, and you won't always have the information that reveals the anger is inappropriate. Try to think about what might be making the person who hurt you act the way they did. Think about what might be going on in their life. If you can give them the benefit of the doubt, if you can generate some compassion, you can learn to let go of the anger.

Letting it go is the most effective way to deal with anger. It should be your ultimate goal.

Stage Three: Bargaining

Bargaining is the third in the list. In this use, bargaining is not negotiating your divorce, it's the things you do when you are trying to make the situation go away. “I'll change; I'll do this or stop doing that.” *Anything*, you promise, *but please don't go through with it.*

You bargain when you think you can do something to stop the madness. It’s not the same as reconciliation, where you leave the door open to resolution or even reuniting. Bargaining can lead to wild promises and persistent badgering in the hope that the other party will reconsider.
It is the offspring of desperation. If taken to extremes, it can lead to lawsuits and restraining orders. It's the futile efforts of someone unwilling to let go.

Stage Four: Depression

Depression is the fourth stage, but it can wind through each stage or come and go during the process.

It's important to mention here that there is a big difference between temporary depression and clinical depression. If you are feeling so down that you can't shake it, if it's been going on a long time or you are entertaining thoughts of suicide, you must seek professional advice. There are tools, medication and strategies designed to combat serious and debilitating depression. There is help available, so don't hesitate to reach out for it.

However if you are not at this extreme end of depression, chances are you are going through the type of depression everyone struggles with at one point or another in their lives. My experience has been that, of the five stages, anger and depression are two that hit everyone. We've already looked at anger, let's look at depression.

For some people, depression is anger without the energy. For me, depression is what's left when the anger isn't present. In my case, depression feels emotionless. It's a black hole. I simply don't care. I don't want to move, to take care of myself, to make an effort to do anything.

When I see the abyss looming, I know to take action.

Immediately.

Prayer is an anchor for me. My mind stills when I am in conversation with God. Then I'm ready to apply techniques I've learned about managing depression and other mind-based challenges.

It's a four-part approach. Recognize your thoughts, control them, redirect them, replace them.

If you are hounded by pessimistic thoughts, try giving yourself a time out. Take a 30-minute block of time when you don't allow any negative thought to occupy your mind.

If you can't do it for 30 minutes, try 15. If you succeed at 30, up it to 60. In the same way that your body grows stronger when you exercise the muscles, your mind will get better at managing your thoughts when you practice. For some, the concept of being able to direct your thoughts is ground-breaking. Yet it's a skill we can all acquire.

Once you are competent at banishing negative thoughts for

a time, try turning it on its head. Instead of allowing yourself islands of time for no bad thoughts, start to shepherd them to an island of their own. Set aside an interval each day when you will entertain negative thoughts. Then only allow them to appear when scheduled. If they try to invade your mind at other times, gently remind them they have a designated playing field and they're banned until then.

There's a growing suspicion that our changing roles in society contribute to the increasing numbers of depressed people. The idea is that we no longer spend much time in physical labor, and we don't get the satisfaction of working with our hands to produce results that enrich our lives.

Meaningful physical activities boost neurochemicals in our brain that contribute to feelings of well-being. Gardening, auto repair, knitting – even exercise – can accomplish this as long as it's perceived as *meaningful to you*. These activities, within the context of your life, increase levels of serotonin and endorphins.

Moving our hands activates a larger area in the brain than moving other parts of the body, such as the legs or torso.

Our push-button lifestyle denies us opportunities to create manually and produce useful results unless we seek them out. Try to incorporate some physical activity that is worthwhile to you into your regular schedule.

Regular exercise of all kinds also has proven benefits as a depression-fighter. The Mayo Clinic suggests exercise can increase levels of neurotransmitters and endorphins, reduce immune system chemicals and elevate body temperature, which is thought to have a calming effect.

Additionally, they point out, exercise improves self-confidence, breaks the cycle of negative thoughts, increases the ability to cope and expands social circles.

Journaling is another valuable tool. It's simply keeping a diary of your thoughts and feelings. There was a study done in 1994 at Southern Methodist University involving about 50 employees who had been terminated abruptly from jobs that many had held for decades. They were given a pink slip and escorted out of the building with no prior warning. The psychologist who conducted the research commented that he'd never worked with subjects as bitter and angry as these people.

He divided them into three groups, telling the first to keep a diary recording how they spent their day, the second to write their honest feelings about their situation and the third group wrote whatever they wanted. Each group was to spend 20 minutes a day, every day, for a week. The results were surprising. The group who expressed their emotions did much better in securing new jobs, even though all candidates tried equally hard and had a similar number of interviews.

Since then, numerous studies have confirmed the fact that expressing your negative emotions through writing can help healing and recovery. The writing should focus on a difficult or problematic situation, especially if it's something that is eating at you and you might not want to discuss with anyone else.

The best results come when you ask yourself three questions: *What happened, how do I feel about it and why do I feel this way?*

Write from the heart. This isn't going to be seen by anyone but you. Neatness, sentence structure, grammar, spelling – none of these are important. Write for 10-20 minutes daily, describing the situation or telling the story. You don't need to do this forever. You can journal this way, using the three questions, just when you feel especially challenged.

The act of relating it helps you analyze things, even without consciously doing so, and is proven to be more effective than thinking or reflecting on it in your mind. Be sure to be honest, laying out the facts as they are. If you are uncomfortable with having your deepest thoughts on paper, you can burn or shred the documents later.

PINBALL EMOTIONS

The first few years I ricocheted between anger, denial and depression. Like a wild animal trapped in a cage, I threw myself at the bars and paced the floor of my emotions. I wanted out of this place of agony and desolation. I had gotten better at making it through each day, but scratch the surface of my composure and my emotions would flow like blood from a wound. I couldn't live like this.

As I learned more about divorce, I found facts that eased my mind.

I was normal. My highs and lows, my unexpected crying, my

anger were not signs I was dysfunctional or insane. They were typical reactions to a devastating event.

I needed support from people who had gone through divorce and emerged victorious. I was able to connect with others who were struggling with the same issues and we shared our experiences.

This was important, because I continued to have the most wonderful events marred by ugly reality. My younger daughter was getting married to a terrific man. It was a bittersweet moment. I would be the mother of the bride, and like the cheese, I stood alone. In a celebration of marriage and couples, everyone would be paired up but me.

The idea of being so obviously alone at such a important event pierced me anew yet I loathed myself for thinking of me on her special day. I prayed earnestly, and gathered my support system close. My cousins and uncle flew out to be with us, my friends reached out, and I knew I could do it.

By now, my daughters and I had made significant progress in rebuilding our relationship. They were sensitive to my distress, and supportive. That meant a lot.

There were awkward moments, but I think everyone involved was determined to make the day special, in a good way, and leave happy memories. It turned out perfect: The bride was radiant, the maid-of-honor (my older daughter) was beautiful and the grandchildren were precious. The groom was pretty dashing, too.

Whew. I had made it through without embarrassing myself or my family. I had come a long way in surviving trying times.

Good thing, because there was much more to come.

The following year my mother and my only remaining living aunt both fell down and broke their hips within a week of each other. They lived in California, in different towns, and my mother was on the floor for days. I called repeatedly, but in the past, she'd often ignore my calls, so I wasn't worried at first. I tried my useful trick of calling early or late so she'd answer the phone before she remembered she wasn't taking my calls, but could never reach her. Then I began to worry. I sent the police, who broke in and found her on the floor.

My daughters and I got my mother and aunt both relocated to the Bozeman area and settled in health care facilities. My aunt recovered, then began to have fainting spells. Within months she was diagnosed with cancer. Her faith in God was a testimony to everyone, and I felt privileged to be able to be her advocate and support through her ordeal. My daughters and I grew close again as we focused on making her last days as pleasant as possible. She passed away that December.

By the time my aunt died, my mother had made a good recovery. My daughters and I turned our energy into trying to make her comfortable and happy. I was able to move back to Bozeman, my fifth move in four years, but it was a dream come true. I continued facilitating DivorceCare sessions, learning new things every time I went through the program. Principles that applied not only to divorce, but to living a healthy life.

I was making baby steps. I had come to the point where I knew I had to manage my feelings and move beyond my pain or else it would become the thing that defined me. My younger daughter gave me a virtual push when she told me she'd like to throw a surprise party for her sister's birthday. The surprise for me was that she was inviting her father, his wife and their child and wanted me there, too.

It had been five years since our divorce. It was time and I knew it. Nevertheless, my initial response was no. I couldn't imagine how I would get through it.

After about 15 minutes, I called back. *Okay*, I said. *I'll be there.*

She shared her plans with me as she made the arrangements and I was delighted to see how excited she was to do this for her sister, and to bring the entire family together for a fun evening. Children, no matter their age, long to reconnect their parents, even if it's simply as friends, and I admitted to both of them that I knew it was time. I rehearsed mentally how I would handle it. I visualized being gracious and composed.

I was scared to death. The thought of facing my ex and his wife sat like a dread-covered rock in my stomach, but I was determined to push through. I knew forgiveness was the key to my freedom. I knew that as long as I harbored resentment and bitterness, I was never going to have a complete life. I could not move beyond my divorce with unforgiveness in my heart. Like the kid with his hand in the cookie jar, until I let go, I was stuck.

Not forgiving was not an option. Fortunately I had some excellent tools. In DivorceCare I'd learned that forgiving didn't mean forgetting. That by letting go of my resentment I was not condoning the act or indicating that it wasn't devastating. I also learned I didn't have to march up to him and announce I'd forgiven him. It was a decision between me and God.

Knowing these things was a relief. I didn't want to have to say it to his face for several reasons. One, what if he didn't accept it? I would look like a fool and I might retract my decision. That would hurt me and stunt my growth. Secondly, it was clear from my research that forgiving is not a magic wand. I might have to forgive and re-forgive many times. I didn't want someone tallying my restarts and questioning my resolve.

Just like losing weight, it's personal. And while the result is visible to everyone, they don't need to know the process, or the times you fell off the wagon, or how long it really took. God knew I'd decided. He would give me the strength to see it through. I was ready. I was praying and working toward my goal.

Again, life took an unexpected turn.

The party was planned for November.

In September my ex-husband killed himself.

Suicide is unfathomable. When someone who is cold sober sets out to end their life, it leaves behind family who can't imagine how it came to this point. You might wonder what you could have done, what you should have said, but the hard fact is that you can't stop it if they are determined.

So much of our lives take place in our minds. What tragically ruins one person is a bump in the road to another. There is no one in your head but you and God. And if you don't let him in, you are truly alone in the worst sense of the word. Without any safe harbor, your thoughts can convince you that up is down, right is wrong, and suicide is the only way out.

Yet I still questioned. Could a human being have stopped this? After much reflection, I've concluded that I don't think so. The damage was done; the die was cast once he reached the point where he decided this was his answer. Along the way maybe things could have been done differently that might have affected the outcome. But that, too, is now irrelevant.

Before his death, I'd thought I no longer loved my ex-husband. I thought the divorce had severed our connection. It was foolish, because we had been together for 31 years from the time we first went out.

When he died, I discovered a whole new level of grief.

I'd never have the chance to mend the fences. I'd never be able to talk to him about our grandchildren, our children, their lives. Even though he'd remarried I had always believed we would be friends again one day. After all, we had so much shared history. We grew up together, 16 and 18 years old when we began dating, and although there had been trouble in the later years, we had decades of great times.

I still loved him and it ripped me apart. I didn't love him as a wife anymore, but as a lifelong friend, my first love. I realized that forgiveness and death both revealed the truth of what I had denied. If I had never forgiven, I would not have known how much I loved him. Without knowing that I could never move on.

When the only man you've loved dies, and you're the ex-wife, there's no place for you or your grief. The new wife of a few years is the one who gets the sympathy, the support, the comfort. I was given the news in the morning and shortly thereafter my daughters told me they were going to the town where their dad had lived and stay with his wife.

Did I want to come?

If I'd learned anything about grieving, it was that I didn't want to be alone in the face of overwhelming tragedy. So, feeling again like Alice-through-the-looking-glass, I boarded my dogs, packed a bag and headed to my dead ex-husband's house.

I can't even tell you how strange it was. Many people didn't even know who I was. It was like I had been eliminated from the family tree. What shocked me was, other than my daughters, their husbands and a few close friends, no one expected me to be upset. After all, we were divorced, the strangers reasoned. As if that legal document amputated my emotions and erased our history.

Hurt upon hurt assailed me. I was pain on two legs. I was dispatched on errands, such as picking up my ex-husband's wife's mother at the airport. I helped write the obituary, but I was excluded from the funeral home.

What's the protocol? Miss Manners herself might have been stumped.

My daughters and I spoke at the service, but we spoke to a roomful of people who had known him for a few years. Our family's background and memories were something only a handful of us shared, and the rest had no idea who the real man had been. It was surreal.

If I had not been on my way to forgiveness I would have felt so much worse. I do, at times, wish I had been able to accelerate my process, but God knows I was moving in the right direction as fast as I could. He knows my heart. And that's enough.

Stage Five: Acceptance

The fifth stage of grief is acceptance. Acceptance is situational, and you find you accept some things and deny or get angry about others. Ultimately, complete healing requires acceptance across the board, but the journey isn't without ups and downs.

Once you begin to accept your reality you can start to reclaim your life. In the intense healing stage, it feels like you don't own your life. So many things are out of your hands, so much of it is like being swept along a narrow river during spring run-off. You are carried along, trying to keep your head above water, unsure as to your ultimate destination. You only want to survive.

As you move into acceptance, the river widens and slows. You feel less like a piece of flotsam and more like a little boat. You find time to notice things, consider your surroundings, think about something besides making it through one more day.

Progress means going from simply remaining afloat to looking for oars. You have the desire to steer a bit, to make some decisions about your course. The river flows on to the sea, where an ocean of opportunities for victorious living await. Eventually you'll want to upgrade to a sail, rudder or an engine. It all depends on what kind of a sea-worthy craft you will become.

The last section of this book addresses how you shape your boat. Right now we're going to finish looking at how you embrace acceptance.

FLAWED BUT FORGIVEN

I've made a ton of mistakes in my life. There are so many things I would do differently, knowing what I know now. Part of my anger and my bitterness was directed inward. Every time I would act in a way contrary to how I wanted to act, I'd berate myself. It seemed the harder I tried, the worse it got.

I was trying to be godly and I was failing miserably.

Then my research led me to see that beating myself up was counterproductive. It was a form of pride. I knew God wanted me to forgive others, I knew God forgave me, but I held myself to a different standard. I could not forgive myself, and that was wrong.

By not forgiving myself, by letting guilt infect my life, I kept the focus on me. As long as I was thinking of me, there was not much room to think about God or others. Self-loathing is not a virtue, it's a sin.

The commandment to forgive does not exclude you. God does not have different standards for forgiveness, he has one. Forgive. You are forgiven, so likewise forgive.

Everyone.

That means you, too.

It's important to take responsibility for what we've done wrong, but nothing is to be gained by castigating yourself. The Bible, John 8:1-11, NLT, explains Jesus' attitude toward this.

One day, at the temple, he met a group of religious scholars. These men were always trying to trap Jesus with the rule of law. They had a woman who had committed adultery and brought her before Jesus. The law decreed death by stoning, a horrible fate. Jesus had a reputation for compassion. The scholars demanded an answer. "What do you say, Jesus? Death for this woman?"

Jesus said, "Fine, but let the one who has never sinned throw the first stone." No one responded. One by one they went away until Jesus and the woman were alone.

Then he stood up again and said to the woman, "Where are your accusers? Didn't even one of them condemn you?"

"No, Lord," she said.

Then Jesus said, "Neither do I. Go and sin no more."

When the topic of forgiveness is introduced in DivorceCare, often a wall goes up, which is understandable. If you've been hurt, you might not want to forgive. In fact, forgiveness might be the last thing you want to do.

One stumbling block is that, somewhere along the line, the words forgive and forget became inextricably linked. People don't want to forgive because they think it means they will have to forget the offense.

For most people, forgetting would be like pretending it never happened, and that would compound the pain. However the truth is that you can forgive the person without forgetting the memory. The memory of being betrayed or abused is important to help you avoid being put into the same position. Burning your hand on the stove doesn't make you stop cooking, but it certainly teaches you to approach the activity differently. The memory helps us protect ourselves.

Even when you know you don't have to forget, it can still feel like forgiving minimizes what happened. I've heard people say it's like giving the other person a 'get out of jail free' card or a pass on the devastation they've caused. One woman told me it seemed to her like forgiving was the same as saying she wasn't really hurt, that what was done wasn't important. By extension, it made her feel like forgiving would be saying *she* wasn't important.

Another aspect of forgiveness that stops people is the idea that they have to confront the person who hurt them and tell them that they are forgiving them. While this might be useful in certain situations, the act of forgiving is between you and God. He's the one who is interested in the state of your soul and the attitude of your heart.

You can forgive and never see the person again. Interestingly, the act of forgiving causes ripples that change things in ways you will never know. Forgiving frees your spirit and as you lay down the burden of resentment and revenge, there are repercussions all along your life and the lives of others.

Telling the person directly that you forgive them can occasionally have negative consequences. It opens the door to a kind of 'holier than thou' attitude, which is at odds with what God intends for us when we honestly forgive. This can make the other person angry, especially if they believe they don't need to be forgiven, and can escalate problems instead of resolving them. It might also set up expectations that the other person will recognize their transgressions and repent, or be grateful for the forgiveness. When that doesn't happen, both parties feel worse than before the conversation occurred.

You can forgive the person without confrontation and without condoning or dismissing the hurtful act. Now that you know what forgiveness is not, let's see what it is.

What is forgiveness?

Forgiveness is letting go of the resentment and giving up any desire for vengeance. While you are not erasing the memory of what happened, you are releasing the power it has over you. You are freeing yourself from the tyranny of the event.

It's been said that bearing a grudge is like taking poison and waiting for the other person to die. It destroys you while having little or no effect on the offender. Resentment eats away at you.

Revenge can hurt you and your target. However, the desire for revenge is common, because when you're hurt your first impulse is to retaliate.

You'd like the person who caused you pain to recognize just how terrible their actions were and how much damage they caused. In a perfect world, they would feel remorse and beg forgiveness. Unfortunately, in the real world, the injuring party is usually so wrapped up in the pursuit of their own desires they aren't capable of recognizing the pain they've left in their wake.

That can cause you to want to force them to acknowledge it, and can lead to behaving in a way that unleashes the virtual poison of resentment to race through your veins, killing relationships and destroying your peace of mind.

You might resort to telling everyone, especially people who had been friends with both of you, about just how awful your ex-spouse is. You might try to convince your children to take sides. You might treat yourself badly, hoping that the whole world will see how their actions have ravaged you and condemn them.

In the depth of your pain and frustration, you might become physically destructive to your ex or yourself.

Bitterness and hostility take over your life, and you feel justified nurturing your pain because it seems like no one else notices how your life has been ruined. If your former spouse goes on with their life, you might feel like you are replaceable, that you have no value and no significance.

When your life becomes all about the injustice, you miss the joy in daily living. You reject anything positive or pleasurable because it doesn't fit with the identity you've embraced of the suffering victim. This infects your relationships, and when people pull away, it reinforces your negative beliefs about yourself and world. You become isolated and depressed.

The wonderful thing is, while refusing to forgive can spiral you into a dark and terrible place, you have the power to change the entire picture. Forgiving will open your life to possibilities, opportunities and peace of mind.

How do you forgive?

Forgiveness is not a feeling. You don't have to wait until you are in the mood to step into forgiveness. Forgiving begins with a decision.

Sometimes making the decision is too much of an initial leap.

You might have to start with a baby step. You might begin by asking God to help you want to forgive.

You know that forgiveness is the key to everything you hope your life will become. God has commanded us to forgive. We are forgiven ourselves in direct proportion to how forgiving we are to others. This is not a trivial thing.

Yet it is one of the most difficult things for people to do. Letting go of the need to see justice done, to see the scales balanced is nearly impossible at times.

The first step is to acknowledge that you've been hurt. By taking time to recognize and confirm your feelings, you won't be so driven to convince others. Come before God and lay out your pain, your sense of injustice, your frustration.

He knows everything that has happened to you and he knows your innermost thoughts. You can tell him your honest feelings, even if they're ugly. He can bear the weight of your sincere confession and by taking it to him, you will be able to take the action he wants you to in order to heal and find peace.

You don't need to cower in the dark with your pain and your hurt. You are valuable and precious, and God wants to hear your heartfelt emotions. You might try to hide them at work or at home, but with God you can be genuine and real.

The next step is to understand that whether you do it now or later, you must forgive in order to truly live. God commands it, but like so many things God-related, science is also recognizing the importance of forgiveness. It's lovely to know that doing God's will not only pleases him, but has amazing positive effects on you.

Forgiveness training has been studied by Stanford University because of the favorable effects on quality of life, conflict resolution and physical health. Forgiveness becomes easier the more often it's practiced, and has measurable benefits such as lower blood pressure, reduced stress levels, stronger immune system and improved social interaction.

Once you accept that forgiveness is not negotiable, you are ready to take the next step. Find compassion for your offender. The person who hurt you may be hard-hearted, selfish and unrepentant. They may be continuing to cause you pain daily. But they are human, made in the image of God himself.

There is something there you can discover that will help you see that they are not entirely bad. Seek the good and allow yourself to accept that the person who treated you so poorly has suffered in their own life and has also experienced pain and loss. It may even be what drove them to cause pain for you.

Pray for them. It's a transforming act. By praying for your enemies and those who have wronged you, you are moving from victim to victor, and partnering with God to bring about change in your life, their life and the lives of everyone touched by the situation.

A warning here. As you experience the resentment falling away, you might feel emotionally naked. If you've hung on to your anger and bitterness for a long time, it's become a comfortable burden, a familiar encumbrance. When your load is lightened, and the chains of hatred no longer hinder your steps, it's going to feel strange and maybe even uncomfortable. It might be unsettling.

It's hard to accept that you can be free, that you can focus on what you *can* do, not what you've been subjected to. You might want to run back to the shelter of the pitiful identity you created to cope.

Don't.

You deserve more than a life devoted to measuring wrongs, seeking retribution, or evening scores. Leave the ultimate justice to God. You have more important things to do.

And if you don't know what those things are, it's time to start asking. God's created you for a purpose and destiny.

Divorce is not that destiny.

His plan includes hope and a future.

It's time to for you discover it.

Section Three
~Mobility~

Mobility:
The state of being in motion,
the ability to move freely and easily

Get moving!

My metaphorical broken leg is healing, so the doctor prescribes physical therapy. While I may want to stay on the sofa, at this point refusal could make the muscles wither and atrophy.

It's time to get up and begin rehabilitation. The painful, but important, exercises will restore my leg to its pre-broken stage or even improve it.

If I avoid it or do the minimum, I'll pay the price with reduced mobility and limited capacity. In order to be effective, I need to be committed to restoring my health and willing to put forth the effort.

Physical therapy for your heart is similar. It requires pushing past the pain, even when you want to settle for being "good enough".

When you're first divorced, it takes everything you have to manage your life, your emotions and the demands of living.

As I said before, I was hopeless in those early days. I couldn't envision a future, I had no ability to dream. My devastation consumed me.

Even small everyday chores drained me. After the bankruptcy and divorce I couldn't go to the mailbox without getting sick to my stomach. So much bad news came in letters and notices, it took years before I could pick up mail without a sinking feeling in my gut.

I had to force myself to go out in public. I didn't want to be seen. I wore a tough facade, a shield that was supposed to protect me from the slings and arrows, but it also kept me from sunlight and friendship and wholeness.

Eventually I rebelled against my self-imposed prison. I despised living in fear and constant worry. I knew God didn't want this for me. I also knew that by hiding in the shadows, I was demonstrating weak faith in my Creator.

But I still battled feelings of worthlessness and failure. I wanted to give up.

Fortunately, God hadn't given up on me.

His value system is so different than ours. Humans like to rank the quality of life by status, power or wealth, assigning significance in relation to position on that scale.

It's a flawed measuring system. You know people who are rich but miserable, and others who are financially strapped but joyful. Peace can't be bought with money, and joy isn't a result of influence. Yet we keep thinking they are cause and effect.

In God's eyes, my worth was never in question. Saved by grace, I didn't need to "qualify" or earn my place, my place was assured. With that kind of validation, how could I settle for a tepid existence, a pale echo of a full, satisfying life?

Just like with physical therapy, it wasn't going be without effort. I had to take an active role. Being a part of my own recovery was crucial.

I was not a victim of circumstances, instead I was a force for change.

Instead of dwelling on what I'd lost, I decided it was time to take inventory of what I still had.

Time to count blessings.

To begin with, I had God, who loved me unconditionally. I could appreciate who I was because I was made in the image of perfection, and I was loved.

I had two incredible daughters and we were close again, something that was worth more than a pile of gold to me.

My daughters had wonderful husbands, precious children and lovely in-laws.

I had dogs that amused me and provided unquestioning companionship.

I had a roof over my head and a car to drive.

The list grew. It was clear I had a great deal to be thankful for, and much to sustain me as I moved forward.

My goal had evolved from surviving to moving beyond divorce and discovering my authentic life.

Authentic is defined as genuine, honest, trustworthy and faithful. Everything I longed to be.

The very things God wants for us.

You can't get there unless you are completely honest and transparent with yourself and God.

When people think of honesty, they usually put it in terms of others. Being honest with friends, family, associates. But sometimes the most difficult place to be honest is in your own mind.

You can't make changes if you don't see things as they are. You can't grow. You'll be stuck. Facing the truth can be tough, and we dodge it by being too busy, or fogging our brains with alcohol, drugs or food. It's exhausting.

We deceive ourselves by thinking if we keep it hidden, it's hidden from God as well, and if we're honest with him, God will condemn and possibly abandon us. But the truth is,

God's on your side. He wants you to bring him your worst and give it over without reservation. You can trust him.

In Psalms, David asks God to search his heart and his anxious thoughts. Do the same. Let him ferret out those buried fears and private shortcomings, so he can redeem them. *Redeem* is a wonderful word that means *absolve, deliver from, save.*

God can free you from the tyranny of secrets. He wants to clear the debris so you can thrive and glorify him with your life. There's no glory in being a fearful, terrified person hiding under the bed.

Lay your burdens at his feet and ask his forgiveness. Then, like the woman at the well, go forward and sin no more.

Don't despair if you've messed up in life. Your experience, mistakes and tough times shape you. If you allow God to use them, you'll find you have a deeper understanding of others, with wisdom and compassion you wouldn't otherwise possess.

Revelation can bring renovation. However, not every discovery is earthshaking or immense. The minor truths you uncover can make a positive difference, too. Even something as simple as realizing you keep a whirl-wind social schedule because you hate being alone.

I had a friend who used to double-book herself regularly. This led to misunderstandings, hurt feelings, and scuttled friendships.

If you asked her, she didn't know why she did it. She'd claim she was disorganized or too busy or lost track of appointments. After really drilling down to the truth, she realized she didn't want to be alone. Yet she was driving away her friends with what they saw as her inconsiderate attitude toward them.

By being honest with herself, she could form a new strategy, one that wouldn't result in bringing about the very thing she feared.

When you stop hiding from yourself, you can make better choices.

SIMPLIFY

It's hard to thrive in chaos, but it often seems like people choose things that make their life more difficult instead of easier.

Although it baffles me, I have to admit I've done it myself. We throw roadblocks in our own way, then complain because nothing's working out right.

Mini acts of self-sabotage. The little things we allow or neglect that make our lives more difficult.

A psychologist could dissect it and I imagine there are reasons that tie into self-worth, reluctance to treat ourselves well, even perhaps some backwards payoff for suffering through our own incompetence.

Fortunately, we don't need to understand why to make a change. We only need to recognize the problem area then invest a little time to analyze it and come up with a solution. It might be obvious, once you stop and think about it.

I was at an event where a speaker was telling stories on himself to illustrate this. He explained he could never find his car keys. Every time he had to go out, he'd waste valuable time looking for them, missing appointments because he'd have to turn his house upside down in order to find his misplaced keys.

He was apologizing, yet again, for being late when his friend asked him why he didn't make a place for his keys and put them there every time he came into the house?

He was telling the story to point out that it didn't take a genus to figure it out, just someone who recognized the problem and applied logic. It revolutionized his daily routine. It also made him realize he was the one making his departures hectic and chaotic.

Solutions don't have to be complicated. There are many little changes you can make to help yourself throughout the day. Businesses hire efficiency experts for tips on streamlining and improving their productivity and you can be your own efficiency expert by examining your routine and finding ways to refine it.

Thinking in new ways can get you unstuck. For example, I used to insist on writing from beginning to end. My thoughts didn't always cooperate, and my flow of words would get clogged by unwritten ideas.

I'd be blocked. Stopped cold. Frustrated by my desire to keep things linear and logical. I'd push forward, but by the time I got to the place where the ideas belonged, they were long forgotten.

A successful writer friend, author of over 50 books, suggested I take a break when I reached that point, and write that pesky scene or passage, getting it out of my head and clearing my mind to continue. I began to keep a file for sections that would fit at another time, and now I hop on over there and write what's on my mind, then return to my primary project, bypassing the block.

Not a huge change, but extremely valuable, nonetheless.

What are some simple things you can do to make your life less stressful?

When you get to the store, do you forget some of the items you need? Keep a grocery list on your fridge. Paste a pad up there with a pencil and jot down the item as soon as you use it up. Rip off the page and take it to the store. You'll save money and time by buying what you need when you need it.

Put a white board on your fridge and write the important things you must do or take care of that day or the next. I do this with something I don't want to forget but don't want to put in my planner. Trash day, for example. I erase it as soon as I haul the trash to the curb.

Automate your bill-paying. You can do this with just the really important things if you still want the control of writing monthly checks. It relieves your mind when you get sick or go on vacation, knowing you won't forget the rent or mortgage payment.

Don't let your gas tank get lower than ¼ full. It costs the same, you fill up a little more often but don't have deal with driving in a storm at midnight with the needle on empty.

Sit down the first week of December and get your tax stuff in order.

Balance your checkbook.

Are you going somewhere new? Get the directions ahead of time, print out a map if it helps. Leave in plenty of time so you don't set yourself up if you get lost. Make sure you have a jacket, water, a towel, a flashlight, whatever you might need in your particular area to be prepared.

Little things. Things that make you crazy when you don't pay attention to them. Simple steps that will smooth the way and get you through your day with less angst.

Once you've incorporated the easy things, consider going a little deeper. Examine your attitude and see if you are acting in ways that make life more difficult, and if you can rearrange how you function to make things easier.

Let's say you have a desk where you pay your bills, but you don't use it much. The whole bill-paying thing is an unhappy time for you, and the only place that doesn't depress you is when you sit outside in the garden. You like it because of the fresh air, flowers and wild birds. Yet you force yourself to pay bills at your desk, because you have a desk and it's for bill-paying. You've made a rule for yourself and you're going to stick to it.

Instead, why don't you give yourself a break? Get a shoebox or container together with all the things you need to pay bills, such as a letter-opener, stapler, stamps, return-address stamp. Then take this with you when you pay your bills. You have to do it, why not make it as comfortable as possible?

It's not bad to make adjustments that lead to a better experience, yet repeatedly we deny ourselves the benefits of tailoring chores and duties to make things easier.

Another example: you have a nice backyard deck, but you don't spend much time enjoying it. Instead of avoiding it for an entire season, take a look at what keeps you from using it.

In my case, I had the furniture arranged in such a way that it was awkward to barbecue. It made the entire process a trial. In the summer the last thing you want to do is heat up the house, and I'd made it unpleasant to grill, so I'd grab some fast food or even treat myself to a nice restaurant with a friend. The problem was this was expensive and unnecessary. When I rearranged the deck to be more user-friendly, I found myself much more willing to spend time there and entertain friends at my place.

You may think these little things are insignificant, however these situations add up and contribute to the quality of your life. A friend once said: *If you think small things don't matter, try spending the night in a tent with a mosquito.*

Eliminate the aggravation where you can. Conserve your strength for those situations you can't.

RESILIENCE

In my research I was curious about what made some people able to bounce back from adversity while others were crushed. It didn't seem to be based on the circumstances. Resilient people rebounded from devastating situations that sunk their contemporaries.

I found a study done on 10,000 people who were laid off from one large company. Researchers wanted to know why some prospered while others struggled, and they found that those who thrived had three things in common: *They saw problems as challenges, they were committed to facing them head on, and they looked to influence their own outcomes.*

Thinking of a problem as a challenge opens up possibilities. It puts you in charge. It switches you from being frozen, staring at an insurmountable wall of resistance, to someone searching for a ladder, a tunnel or another way around the obstacle.

Once you have redefined the problem as a challenge, confront it directly and believe that you can make a difference through the actions you take.

In the study, researchers found four important pillars that contributed to positive results and a winning attitude, which you can apply to your situation.

FIRST, IDENTIFY YOUR STRENGTHS

Resilient people not only learn from hard times, they acknowledge their own fortitude. Think back to when you accomplished something despite adverse conditions. Recognize that you have the ability and talent to succeed, and that you have succeeded previously. Take note of the strengths you possess that made it possible.

NEXT, SEEK OUT SUPPORT

Find time for what rejuvenates you. Make room in your life for your faith, your friendships, your pets, your garden. Studies show relationships enrich your life, something most of us know without being told. It's up to you to make time to maintain and nurture your friendships.

Friendships can also help you stay connected to your history. One thing that can happen when you divorce, especially if you've been married for a long time, is that you lose the one person who knew you back when, the person who shared your experiences as a couple and a parent.

I met my husband when I was in high school. He taught me to drive a stick shift, he took me to prom and bought me my first steak and lobster dinner. Together, we made two beautiful babies and shared many wonderful major life events.

When he left, I had no one with whom I could remember those times.

You might wonder why this matters.

Numerous studies have found that, rather than being a waste of time or a melancholy habit, reminiscing can improve your sense of well-being. This view of nostalgia has been gaining acceptance over the past thirty years.

Nostalgic memories, scientists found, often feature the individual in a prominent role, and frequently have redeeming elements. The memory might begin with a negative event but it ends on a positive note.

For example, when we moved from California to Montana in the early 80's the prime interest rate was 21 percent. We leased our house, hoping to sell it in a year, when interest rates might be more affordable.

A year later, the renters stopped paying rent and refused to move out. It was a stressful time. We had to pull together, and we worked through it. Finally we were able to sell the California house and, as a result, negotiated a better deal on the house we bought in Montana.

An experience that began badly ended up well. Remembering how you successfully navigated a tough situation reinforces the belief that you will be able to do that again. It's encouraging.

Reminiscing also connects us, strengthening our bonds. Scientists call it "social integration". It fortifies our ties with family and friends, and gives us confidence in their future support.

Scientists differentiate between nostalgia and regular memories. The nostalgic recollections are more complex and evocative, with a positive outcome. Scientists believe that people prone to depression might be helped by recalling nostalgic memories.

It's no surprise, then, that being able to reminisce with friends and family is a crucial part of healing and recovery.

Human support is important, but companionship can come in smaller packages. Pets contribute much to our health and happiness, from lowering stress to keeping us laughing. Research proves pets can add joy to your life. If you're at a place or in a location where you can't make a commitment to a dog or cat, consider a fish, a bird or a guinea pig. Even a bird feeder outside a window can bring a little positive nature into your world.

I have two dogs, and a Betta fish. My dogs are important buddies in my life, and our adventures will be the subject for another book. My fish is the surprise, more engaging than you might suspect. He's a colorful and peaceful presence, who can live for up to four years with proper care.

Bettas, like all creatures, appreciate being where they can be part of your everyday life. Mine is on the counter, where he sees me moving about many times during the day. He responds to activity and eagerly awaits feeding time. I enjoy the minimal effort it takes to provide a healthy environment where he can flourish.

If a live creature is too much for you,consider cultivating some houseplants. They also bring benefits and require minimal, but consistent, attention. It's a great way to get outside yourself. Nurturing something alive is a restorative activity. Start with a plant, with the idea of reaching out to people eventually. It will enrich your life.

THIRDLY, FEED YOUR GROWTH

As you travel the road to recovery, keep in mind the analogy of the broken leg. Proper healing requires not only outside structure and exercise, but internal nourishment through healthy food and nutrients. By the same token, you need a plentiful supply of positive input to enable your recovery.

Spending time each morning meditating on the Bible is a solid way to begin the day and get in the right frame of mind. Memorizing verses that are significant to you also helps you build a foundation of instant reference material you can use to get through rough patches. Quiet prayer is like plugging into the power source, God, and charging up to face the challenges ahead.

Another effective way to feed your recovery is familiar. It's counting your blessings.

A gratitude journal is a proven way to increase your happiness. God encourages us to be thankful and there is plenty of scientific evidence to back it up. In 2003, Dr. Robert A. Emmons did research on gratitude with three groups of people. One group kept track of things they were grateful for, the next group listed things that bothered them and the third tracked things that happened without focusing on whether they were positive or negative. They discovered that the gratitude group was significantly happier. Other studies have shown similar results.

It's simple to incorporate this practice as part of your daily habits. Take a moment at night before you go to sleep, or any other time that works, and list five things for which you are grateful. They can be as basic as the fact you have a place to live, food to eat, a car to drive. They might be a beautiful sunset, a laughing child, or a perfect tomato. Whatever they are, this is your opportunity to recognize and name them.

It's so easy that you might be tempted to skip it. I urge you to try it instead. It takes minutes and is a proven way to refocus. I've found it to be a great antidote to negative and depressing thoughts. When I recognize an undesirable thought coming into my head, I stop and replace it with a quick inventory of five things for which I am truly grateful, pausing to savor and appreciate each one.

This is a valuable practice, but it's not a brick wall. Even when you deliberately consume a diet of mind-healthy input, worries still find their way into your consciousness.

It's only human. Everyone worries from time to time as a response to problems. When it becomes constant, it's not only ineffective, it's damaging.

Worries are negative thoughts about things in the future. Worries spring from a desire to control a situation, as if by thinking about it hard enough you can influence the results. Chronic worriers believe they are being proactive, anticipating every crisis and preparing for the future.

While prudent planning is a responsible activity, worry can hinder your thought process and exaggerate fear and anxiety.

It can weaken your cardiovascular system, dull your emotions or even block your ability to respond to real threats quickly. Just like the little boy who cried "wolf", when you need to deal with a legitimate danger, your body won't recognize the urgency.

Serial worriers see the world as unsafe and are plagued with negative thoughts. Dwelling on these thoughts reinforces them, and there's a very real danger that the mind will replay the negative to a point where it becomes all-consuming and more real than the true situation. Sufferers struggle to manage their emotions and the world around them, but the more they try, the more pervasive the worry.

You've probably heard of the experiment where you don't think of a pink elephant. A large, pink elephant is absolutely not supposed to be in your head right now. Shiny pink toenails, pink flapping ears, long pink trunk.

Perhaps all you can think of now is that annoying pink elephant.

It's like that with negative thoughts. The more you try to banish them, the more stubbornly they persist.

It's been documented that the mind and body is able to process actual disastrous events better than anticipated catastrophes. In other words, you can't solve something that hasn't happened, regardless of how imaginative you are. Thinking about bad things that might come about does not give you the power to change the future, or even mitigate the damage.

The Bible says it well in Matthew 6, telling us that we should not worry about tomorrow, because tomorrow will worry about itself. Each day has enough trouble of its own. You can only affect actual events and problems as they arrive. You can't fix that which hasn't yet occurred, nor alter that which is in the past.

So what can you do when worries attack? There are steps you can take to manage your unwanted thoughts. These are the same steps that work on anxieties, worries and depression. This is what I've learned to do.

First, I pray to calm my mind, connect with God and open myself to the possibilities. Then I assess the situation. If there is action I can take to change things or eliminate the problem, I make a plan and implement it. If there's nothing I can do, then I release it to God. Not as easy as it sounds, but worth the effort. He is strong enough to take on the worst troubles and he's willing. There's no better place for your worries than at God's feet.

Sometimes, despite my best efforts, the thoughts return. I write down unproductive worries as they occur to me, but postpone thinking about them until a designated time. I allow myself to think about them within the framework of that "worry time". Often when the appointed hour arrives, I'm either no longer interested in thinking about them or the situation has become a non-issue.

If the worries are persistent and troublesome, I journal. I do this off and on as needed to clear emotions and intense feelings, especially when I don't want to broadcast them.

Then I shred the journal pages, because in order to be brutally honest on paper, I need to know it will never be seen.

When I journal, I pose the questions: *What's the worst thing that could happen? Could I survive it?* I've survived worse, in most cases. I've survived things I never would have imagined. Then I think back to what I was worried about last year, or three years ago. If I can remember it, I find that most of it never came to pass.

I stay grounded. Just like Jesus said in Matthew, I remind myself that it's fruitless to worry about tomorrow. I ask, *Am I okay, right now, this minute, in this place?* The answer is usually yes, because what's obsessing me is the "what if's" rather than the current situation. So I coach myself to stay mentally in the present moment and quit creating imaginary disasters that my mind is not able to process nor solve.

Then I think about five things I'm thankful for, and I do it with consideration and thought, not flippantly. By counting my blessings, I refocus on how much I do have, and that usually leads to a heartfelt prayer of gratitude and gets me back on track.

As you become skilled in managing yourself, and taking control of your emotions, you'll reach a new level in your growth and recovery.
For me, I knew I'd come to this juncture when I felt a desire to do more than cope with my challenges, I wanted to make something of my life. I'd traveled the path from hopeless to hopeful, from despair to expectation. I knew I'd be okay, but what about people who were where I had been, who needed

to find their way?

Could my experiences be useful?

It had to count for something. I could extend a ladder to those in the pit I had been in, and offer the hope I had been so desperate to find.

So the question becomes, now that *you* are on your way, what is the next step going to be? Your life can make a difference, your experiences matter. You have much to contribute and a unique place to fill in the world.

What will your life look like?

Be assured, no matter your age or your circumstances, you have unique talents and gifts to share. Take Corrie Ten Boom, for example.

Corrie was a Holocaust survivor. She was born in Holland, and as a devout Christian, she provided a hiding place for Jews during the Nazi persecutions of World War II, risking her own safety. Her entire family was arrested and sent to a notorious death camp after being betrayed by a man who had come to her for help.

In the concentration camp, depression and hopelessness threatened to overwhelm her, but Corrie continued to worship God. She obtained a Bible and led secret prayer meetings in the midst of the terrible conditions and despite deadly consequences. She said, "Never be afraid to trust an unknown future to a known God." And she lived those words.

During this time, her father and sister died, but a clerical error released Corrie one week before all the women her age were put to death, and, as a free woman, she continued to spread the word of God through broadcasts and personal ministry.

Corrie knew worry and fear, on a much greater scale than anything I'd ever faced, yet she persevered, believing God would bring her through her horrific experiences. "Let God's promises shine on your problems," she said.

But it went beyond survival. Corrie, age 53 when she was freed, spent the rest of her life sharing her love for God and inspiring others with her faith. She set up rehabilitation centers, traveled to 60 countries, produced five films and wrote nine books, one of which is *The Hiding Place*, the story of her arrest and time in the concentration camp. She died at the age of 91.

What are you going to do for the rest of your life?

Do you think you're too old? Too poor? Too uneducated?

Don't waste time making excuses, instead, make history. Prepare yourself for your opportunities. Learn what you need to know. Trust the God who created you to use you to make a difference.

"When a train goes through a tunnel and it gets dark," Corrie said, "you don't throw away the ticket and jump off. You sit still and trust the engineer."

Corrie went through some dark tunnels. She didn't jump off. She didn't let her worries, her fears, her age or physical limitations derail her, and God used her to bless scores of people in His name.

I have a coffee cup with one of her quotes on it. "*Worry does not empty tomorrow of its sorrow: it empties today of its strength.*"

Good advice. Reject your fears and worry, and claim God's promises and strength. In Corrie's words, "It is not my ability, but my response to God's ability that counts."

How will you respond? How will you use the worst of times to make a difference?

PASSIONS

The direction you take today and in the future may be influenced by your passions. Perhaps you don't know what those are, or what talents or skills you possess.

I have some exercises I use with my coaching clients to help them discover what ignites their enthusiasm. One of them is to list ten to twenty things you loved to do when you were a child. What did you enjoy? What did you enjoy about it? Did you do anything unique? Odd? Different than your contemporaries?

These are clues to your interests and strengths. If you want to do more research on your own, there are numerous personality tests available in books and on the Internet designed to help. Search the terms gift assessments, strengthsfinder tests, temperament tests or personality profiles to find them online.

God gave you passions, strengths and interests as part of your personal makeup. Those gifts were meant to be used for his glory and your happiness. Doing what you love makes work seem like play and gives you a reason to get up in the morning looking forward to the day.

Find out what brings you joy, then look for ways to incorporate those things into your life.

PITFALLS

As you regain your vitality and enthusiasm for life, you might be tempted to jump into a relationship rather than finishing the work of finding out who you are and discovering your purpose.

If you were sick, and taking antibiotics, you know the danger in throwing them away before you've taken the course just because you're feeling better. Your doctor warned you, when you got the prescription, to take all of them. That's because feeling better doesn't mean you are well, and stopping the medicine could backfire.

It's the same with your healing. You feel better. You feel strong and normal, but you still think that the right person, the right romance, is the answer.

That thinking is your warning sign. It's a paradox. As long as you look to another person to fix you, or complete you, you're not ready for a healthy relationship. You'll be ready when you aren't really looking anymore. When you don't want someone in your life to fulfill it, restore it or make you feel whole.

Continue building your same-gender friendships and invest in learning about you, connecting with God and discovering your unique contribution.

As you reconnect with society, be sure to choose friends who are good for you. It might shock you to discover there are some people who don't want you to get well, especially if it means you are going to live differently. They don't want you to give up activities you once shared but no longer enjoy. They don't want to lose their drinking buddy or their gambling pal.

Then there are those who seek out and thrive on being around people when they are vulnerable and weak. Often they are very solicitous, and for a while you believe they are as anxious for you to heal as you are. Then you realize they are very supportive of your fragility but not very happy when you begin to grow stronger. They might sabotage your efforts to be independent.

The majority of people you befriend are not going to be this way. In fact, you might never experience it. But it does exist, and if you sense that someone in your life has an agenda that's counterproductive to yours, examine the relationship more closely.

If you find they're rewarding you for weakness and withdrawing as you move towards health and wholeness, heed the warning signs. If they are someone with whom you spend a lot of time, their manipulation affects your behavior. When you're with them, you're comfortable feeling helpless and uncomfortable when you try to push past it. You may not know why but you find yourself pulling back when you were moving forward in order to maintain the friendship.

The same goes for friends who insist you join them in behavior that you no longer care to do. Friendships like these are not sustainable, unless you stop your progress. Choose a healthy and healed life over one designed to please your friends. True friends will want that for you.

Section Four
~Restoration~

Restore:
To put something back to its original condition, to reinstate, reestablish. To repair, heal, bring back strength and health.

YOU KNOW YOU'VE MADE IT WHEN...

At some point, you will have completed your process of healing. You won't be in the recovery phase any more, you'll be whole again. To revisit the broken leg scenario, you'll be through physical therapy and ready to run the race.

How do you know when you're there?

One indicator of a healthy, whole person is their ability to take criticism and deal with setbacks.

You've known people who seem to grow measurably and others who never change. What's the difference? Part of it is how they handle feedback.

We all get feedback. Every day. The instinctive reaction is to reject it or get upset about it. It's a method we believe keeps us from getting hurt.

Years ago I began learning this, but it's not an easy concept to embrace. It's two steps forward, one step back. It takes practice, but it can yield amazing results.

Here's how it works. The next time someone says something to you that insults your ego, restrain yourself from responding the way you usually do, which might be by denying it or striking back. Just shelve it. Later, when you can examine the comment in private, study it to see if there is any truth in the words. Sift through it like you would pan for gold, letting the water wash away the worthless silt and picking through the rest to see if there is anything of value.

There might be a nugget or flake of golden truth that is painful, but worth considering.

My life's passion is writing, ever since I was a little girl telling stories to the neighbor kids. As an adult I remember an incident when a friend was having success after success, and I was having none. I stumbled and landed in a pothole of envy. As I indulged in a little pity party, someone close to me pointed out that I had no grounds to be jealous. *After all*, they said, *she worked much harder to achieve success than I did, so it was no surprise that the outcome for her was favorable.*

This cut me to the quick. My first response was anger and tears.

After a while – a long while - I thought about it. The delivery had been tactless, but the nugget of truth was there. She did work harder. I couldn't deny it, and what would I achieve by doing so? I could tell myself all day long that my minimal efforts should reap the same rewards as someone putting in two or three times the work, but that didn't change the facts.

I had a choice. Work harder or accept my level of success. Whichever I chose, I was way ahead of the alternative of simply thinking life was unfair and I was doomed to be unlucky. By mining the truth from that hurtful comment, I moved from a victim of circumstances to author of my own fate.

It can be painful. Not every comment contains gold, and I discard plenty, but not before analyzing the words for veracity. The occasional gold flake is priceless, because it's information I might not have realized any other way, and knowing it makes it possible to focus on changing or improving in that area.

Learning to hear feedback and not block it out is a sign of maturity and a direct path to improvement.

Toastmasters International is an organization dedicating to speaking skills, leadership development and self-improvement. The members give speeches regularly and are critiqued each time in order to get better. The weekly meetings give members a chance to take on roles, such as Toastmaster, the leader of the meeting and Timer, who keeps track of the length of the speech. There is also a Grammarian and Ah Counter. This person records the number of times the speaker says *ah, um, you know,* or uses other verbal pauses. There is no penalty other than a recitation of the tally at the end of the meeting.

By becoming aware of the bad speech habits, speakers begin to edit themselves. By recognizing their verbal glitches they begin to eliminate them. That's all it usually takes.

If you want to improve yourself, you need to pay attention to feedback. It's not enough to hear it, you must take action when it's legitimate.

But *only* when it's legitimate. Don't let every careless comment make you think you are in need of work, but do learn to evaluate what you're told and decide for yourself if there is anything you can use in the words. If not, then throw the whole thing out. You don't have to defend yourself or justify the comment if it has no truth to it. You can toss it.

If there is something to it, then think about it. Don't beat yourself up with it, but think about how you can change that thing so it's no longer true. How can you handle yourself or the situation better?

Figure it out, then do it. That's how you improve. It's not a course, a pill or a promise. It's awareness and willingness to change when you must and polish up some dull areas when needed. No one else can do it for you. You're in charge.

CHANGE THE WORLD

Divorce can drain you of everything. You might feel hopeless, you might feel powerless, you might feel like you don't have the energy to change a light bulb, let alone change the world. The beauty of it is, you don't have to change the entire world, just your little corner of it. Do something that makes a difference is someone's life. Reach out to others and you'll find satisfaction that goes beyond what you achieve with personal success.

Get outside yourself.

All this introspection has a place, but it can get tiring when the focus is always on you. As you heal, the need to focus on self begins to recede.

In the beginning you were consumed with surviving. If you have children, they were your next priority. Keeping a roof over your head, performing your job, maintaining a home took every bit of your energy.

As you recovered, you established routines and budgets. You found some stability. Emotionally you have gained ground, created friendships, devotional time, relationships with God and friends that give you firm footing and balance. But you still find too often you are thinking about yourself, pushing away thoughts you don't want to dwell on.

There's something you can do that will turbo-charge your recovery. Something that will create a major, positive shift.

To understand, it helps to look at what drives us. In 1943 Dr. Andrew Maslow wrote an article about human motivation. His conclusions were that humans were motivated first by meeting their survival needs like food, sleep and safety. Only when those were met could they step into social needs like friendships and relationships or esteem needs like accomplishment and self-respect.

At the top of his list was self-actualization, which is when we are motivated by truth, wisdom, justice and meaning. In the Bible, it's plain that God wants us to reach the level where we are motivated and defined by these things. God's plan, of course, revolves around a relationship with him, and it's my belief that we can only reach the pinnacle of our potential when he is in the center of our lives. I know very few people who are motivated by these four characteristics if they are scrambling to glorify themselves, gathering money and power to feed their desires for control and dominance.

As a believer, your value system is different. If you aim to please God, those targets of truth, wisdom, justice and love are directly in your sights. The method for achievement is attainable. Helping others is a proven way to reach the next level. It's fulfilling the ultimate commandment. It's love in action.

The Bible says treat others the way you want to be treated. When I was in the early years of divorce, I craved understanding, knowledge and support. When I found a group program which offered that I began to facilitate it for others. Now, I'm not special, and it didn't take any impressive qualifications. I just knew what it would have meant to me and wanted to make sure that was available to fellow sufferers. And as I mentioned before, I've been as blessed as anyone by the experience.

There is something you, too, can do that will give you satisfaction and a focus outside yourself. Read to children at the library. Help out at the Farmer's Market. Volunteer at Vacation Bible School. Walk and socialize dogs at the local shelter so they can become someone's loyal companion.
Let your interests guide you. Nothing is too small to have an impact. Little things generate outward ripples of love you

can't even fathom. Whatever you do, throw yourself into it. Set out to be the best dog-walker or story reader you can. Set a goal and achieve it. Then set another one.

Volunteering stretches you. It balances you and gets your mind off yourself. When you help someone else, when you do something to make life better for people, animals or the future, you feel wonderful. It's an accomplishment, a success.

Success is how we build self-esteem and grow. If the baby didn't succeed at some of his attempts, if he never got on his feet or never moved forward, he'd quit. But even though he fails some of the time, the successes spur him on. Success in the small things leads to success in the larger things.

Soon you'll begin to have dreams and desires to do something with your rediscovered life. I can remember the feeling I got when hope returned. It was so familiar, so welcome. A twinkle somewhere deep inside, a glimmer of what might be again. I knew I'd turned a corner.

After wandering in the land of confusion for so long I'd come to a new place. I'd rediscovered who I was and what inspired me. When I began to have hopes and dreams about the future, I spent less and less time obsessing about the past, about the divorce and related pain. I began thinking about what purpose God had called me to and what he wanted me to do for others. I knew he wanted me to tell them he loves them, and he has wonderful things in mind for their futures, even if they feel like everyone else has given up on them.

Having a dream is one thing, but taking steps to make a dream happen is another. It takes determination and persistence.

Which you have. And I can prove it to you.

When babies learn to walk, they don't stand up one day and take off. It's a slow process of trial and error. Like I said earlier when I discussed the importance of crawling, these milestones are crucial to optimum development.

I think we can agree that walking is an improvement over crawling and crawling is better than lying on your back staring at the floor. What drives babies to improve their situation? We can't explain how much better it is, and they don't understand the importance of walking, yet healthy babies know. They want to walk.

They see us, so they have role models, but I think they'd want to walk regardless. The joy in a babies' faces when they begin to crawl reveals how powerful and exciting it is to move independently.

The ability to walk doesn't come without effort. They stand, usually with the help of a coffee table or sofa. They fall. They bump their heads, their elbows and knees. They stand again. They fall, sometimes rolling over backward like stranded turtles. They gather up and go at it again.

Where do they get the determination?

What if they gave up? What if every baby, instead of persisting, just quit? After five times, or ten or twenty. They simply said that's it. They would sit and crawl forever. No walking.

Yet we don't see people crawling in the malls, or on the streets. Of those who were capable, every one pushed themselves to walk. We are driven to achieve, despite the setbacks, the failures, the bruises.

I would guess that you probably went through the same maneuvers to walk. And that you have been walking for a while. Even if, for some reason, you aren't walking I'll bet it's not because you quit. You have tenacity in your bones. You can make things happen.

Making your dreams come true is like that. You have to want it enough, and not give up. There is enough about doing that to fill another book, but for this one, know that you have what it takes.

If you fall, and you will, pick yourself up and go at it again. The baby didn't quit, but if he had he would wonder the rest of his life what he was missing. He'd never know if he didn't believe it was possible. He'd never know if he didn't try and try again.

You'll never know what you might miss if you give up too quickly. If you quit trying just because you fell or got hurt. You don't want to stop at the 20th try only to find out later you would have made it at the 22nd.

I've had stops and starts along this path. I've had flagging faith at times, when I've panicked about how God was going to make things work because I couldn't see it. I've bolted from my path, veering off to do things that made more sense to me, like taking full-time work that left no room in my life for divorce coaching, facilitating or connecting with my family and friends. I willfully banished myself to the virtual desert, where I wandered asking *why?* when all I had to do was walk out and resume my work.

So many times I put roadblocks up and banged my head against walls of my own making. God's patient. And he loves me and gently leads me back to where I'm supposed to be if I take his hand and let him.

Divorce is not my destiny. It's an event in my life that had the potential to destroy me or change me for the better. My calling, to comfort others with the same comfort God has given me, is richer and more powerful because of the experiences I've had.

Divorce is not your destiny. The event will fade in your memory but the lessons you learn define who you are in the future. What you are going through today creates the tapestry of what you are becoming. Beautiful patterns, even from ugly threads, when God is the weaver.

GOD IS THE MISSING LINK

We want to be known.
We want to be heard.
We want to be accepted.
We want to be significant.

Consider the cracked pot story, adapted from India folklore.

A water-bearer carried two pots on a yoke across his shoulders. Every day he filled the pots and walked to the master's house.

One pot was cracked and leaked water all along the way, while the other was perfect and didn't spill a drop. After many trips, the cracked pot couldn't stand it anymore and apologized to the water-bearer for his shortcomings.

"I'm sorry I'm not like the perfect pot."

The water-bearer was surprised. "What do you mean?"

"I am unable to deliver a full portion of water, because of my flaws. I make more work for you."

The water-bearer replied gently, "Look along the path. There are colorful flowers on your side because of who you are. There are none on the side of the perfect pot. Your flaws made that beauty possible."

You may be cracked, or chipped or broken, but you have significant contributions yet to make. By trusting in God, improving yourself, forgiving, reaching out to others, you can create beauty and leave a lasting legacy.

No one can travel this path for you. We can go with you, we can point out the potholes and steer you away from the cliffs, but you must walk it out yourself.

My younger daughter graduated with a degree in Psychology. After graduation I asked her what she learned in her studies.

"I learned," she said, "that you can't change anyone. They have to want to change."

If you don't want to change, there is no magic that will make it happen. How you live is up to you. The choice is yours. You can read the books, take the classes, pop the pills, pay the therapist, but no one can do the work it takes to have a life filled with joy, hope and peace. Only you.

I heard Dale Brown speak, and if you don't know who he is, he was the basketball coach with the most wins to his credit in Louisiana State University's history. He coached for 25 years and earned the moniker "Master Motivator". He had many inspirational things to say, but one lodged itself in my mind, probably because I love words so much. He said that in 1806, Webster's dictionary defined success as "fortunate, happy, kind and prosperous", while today's Merriam-Webster online defines it as "the attainment of wealth, favor or eminence".

That sums up how our attitudes have changed. I can't help but wonder what the world would look like if we still believed success was being happy, kind and prosperous instead of attaining fame and fortune. It doesn't take a genius to see the effects of pursuing money and celebrity status today. All you have to do is look at government greed, financial power plays and reality shows.

This life-changing event is a time to take inventory. It's a time to think about what success means to you, and how you want the rest of your life to look. You get to decide what matters and how you define yourself. What you do every day forms your future, in small ways and large ones.

Will you push yourself to try new things? To expand your comfort zone? To reach for the stars?

My trip with the RV and my dogs, which I described in the beginning of this book, was a blast. I spent nine days camping with them, no TV or radio, doing what I love. I wrote, walked along the river, explored a ghost town and took many photographs.

There was a moment of panic early on, when I discovered water leaking from an unknown source and I had a meltdown. All my insecurities washed over me like a bucket of cold water and I sat on the floor of the RV and sobbed.

Who did I think I was? I can't do this! I don't know how to fix anything and now I'm stuck miles from home with no one to help me get this repaired! I can't do this! I was crazy to think I could!

Yes, no matter how far you come, how brave you seem, you'll still face adversity, you'll have doubts and you'll wonder if you can make it. The difference is, these feeling don't last. I've learned, and you will too, how to manage these setbacks and how to bounce back.

I picked myself up, mopped up the water, then used trial and error to find the leak. I did contact my daughters, who listened to my whining and offered their support, but I solved the problem myself.

As you move forward, face these difficulties and resolve them, you'll experience the joy that comes from discovering you are up to the challenge. Confidence comes from achievements, and you can handle it.

With the leak sealed, the rest of the trip was smooth and exceeded my expectations.

When I returned home, I realized I'd arrived. Not at any particular geographical location, but back to a place where I have dreams, energy and enthusiasm for my life.

You will arrive there, too. Don't short-circuit the process. By taking the path of healing and recovery, you'll gain what you need and be prepared when you arrive at your next opportunity. The one that begins a new chapter of your life, the one that has the potential to be more exciting and fulfilling than you ever imagined.

Your destiny.

Afterword

My friend, another Life Coach, talks about books and projects as babies to birth. If that's true, this has been a long gestation. When I started facilitating DivorceCare, I felt the stirrings of a book inside me. It made no sense to me to have gone through all the things I had without being able to use it to help others facing the same challenges.

I found that, just like recovery, you can't rush the process. I have files full of ideas, research, theories and lessons on divorce and recovery gathered over the years. The problem was, I wasn't ready to go public with it yet. I wrote plenty, but it didn't sound right. I was still processing, still venting, still recovering.

I wasn't ready for a new relationship, the one with my reader. I wanted both of us to benefit from our experience together, but my emotions were not quite evolved enough to tell the story from my heart without rancor.

It's been nearly nine years now since my divorce, and many steps, lots of hard work, mistakes and triumphs, but I finally believe I have everything in one place and can offer it to you as a labor of love.

This may sound funny, but my overriding thought, as I wrote each day, was that I love you and want to help you. I don't know you, but you are in my mind. I remember how I felt, and what a blessing it would have been to know someone cared and was willing to share their story, with its faults and flaws, because they didn't want me to flounder like they did.

I eventually connected with the people I needed to, but if I'd had a direct line to some of the information I've brought together here, it would have been a bonus.

So it's my gift to you. My struggle laid out, along with the things I learned, with the genuine desire that you will take comfort and hope from my experiences, my failures and successes.

There is a great deal of advice out there on recovering from divorce, but some miss what I consider the key to complete healing. The God factor. You can progress along the path on your own, and you might think that's good enough. But don't deny yourself the joy, the freedom and sheer delight that total recovery brings.

To revive the broken leg analogy one last time, it's like healing so thoroughly that you can run a marathon. You're strong, your steps are sure, and you are so confident about the soundness of your leg that you don't have to give it a thought. You can concentrate on other things that will make the run enjoyable and satisfying.

This is the life you deserve.

If you've never thought about God as a personal savior, it's time to look into it. You may partner up again with another person, but the ultimate partner is your Creator. The one who knows you, everything about you, loves you and sacrificed his son to give you eternal life. The benefits of accepting Jesus Christ as your savior are not all in some distant future, either. There are daily dividends to giving your life to Jesus.

Yes, you live differently. You make different choices, and sometimes you'll feel like you're missing out on things you had in your old life. But what you get is peace in the troubled times, strength in the storms, the ability to go to sleep knowing you spent the day doing your best in your relationships, your job, your humanity.

The world tells you to spread love, and be kind. It's so much easier when you know you are loved, and that the same God of creation cares for you. It doesn't eliminate tough times, but in the same way that friends sustain you, God will be there on a much grander scale.

You're never alone again. You are loved. You are valued. You are an important part of making the world better. Your recovery prepares you to make a difference.

Don't rush it and don't avoid it. Go through it and grow. Then go forth and live like it matters.

Because it does.

Because *you* do.

Jeremiah 29:11 (NIV)

For I know the plans I have for you," declares the LORD,
"plans to prosper you and not to harm you,
plans to give you hope and a future.

Psalm 103:1-5 (NLT)

A psalm of David.

Let all that I am praise the Lord;
with my whole heart, I will praise his holy name.
Let all that I am praise the Lord;
may I never forget the good things he does for me.
He forgives all my sins
and heals all my diseases.
He redeems me from death
and crowns me with love and tender mercies.
He fills my life with good things.
My youth is renewed like the eagle's!

Visit my website: www.DivorceisnotDestiny.com for
discussion questions for small groups,
reading groups or personal study.
SUBSCRIBE to my site for additional updates and
bonus material.
You can contact me there, too.

~ **Bonus Book** ~

Comfort Verses
for the Divorced Christian

Encouragement and Hope Through the Tough Times

Comfort Verses for the Divorced Christian

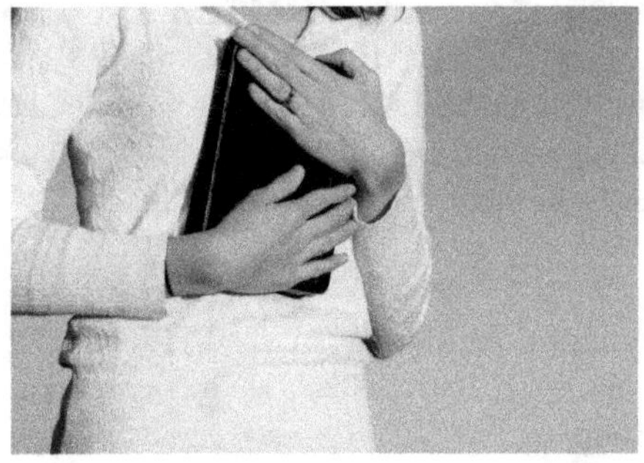

Encouragement and Hope Through the Tough Times

by Lynn Kinnaman

Published by Works by Design Publications,
a division of Works by Design, LLC

... Take hold of my words
with all your heart:
keep my commandments
and you will live.

Proverbs 4:4 (NIV)

Introduction

What are Comfort Verses? They are those Bible verses that sustain us through the tough times, reminding us that God loves us no matter how we've messed up or how hurt we have been. They show us how to live in fullness and joy

When I was going through divorce, I felt alone and lost. My emotions were unpredictable, overwhelming, foreign to me. I didn't know who I was or what to do.

I needed a safe place. I needed to be loved and understood.

I needed comfort.

I discovered there is comfort out there – not the fleeting escape of drugs, alcohol or anything else that obliterates things for a moment – what I found was lasting comfort. Timeless strength.

I knew others could benefit from what I'd learned, so I collected these Comfort Verses for you, so that you, too, can find meaningful support that never fails.

There are four week's worth of daily readings because I like the idea of four weeks – it's a solid, symmetrical time frame.

And frame is a good word in this context. Just like our faith in God is our foundation, spending time reading the Bible provides a framework for a strong life structure. This is *especially* important when you are going through tough times, like divorce.

If you broke your leg, you wouldn't hop right back on it and try to walk or run. You would go through a process that includes a cast, or framework, to protect your leg and help it heal correctly. It's important not to bypass those steps because the result could be additional damage or further injury.

It's the same with your emotional healing.

Over the next four weeks I'm going to ask you to set aside a quiet time each day to meet with God. By the end of this program, you will have created a habit. Your daily routine will include time with God and my hope is you will continue the routine after the 28 days are over.

Each day has a bit of homework or action for you to take. I've made them small, for example, a single item or point to ponder. That doesn't mean you can't expand on my assignment, it just means I want to get you started with a baby step so it's easy to do. I suggest you get a small notebook in which to write, because it's been proven that hand-writing your thoughts can be therapeutic. Typing on the computer is not as effective as putting pen to paper.

It's not easy going through divorce. You may run into other people, even Christians - sometimes especially Christians - who reject you or condemn you because you are divorced.

Remember that human beings, even the best ones, make mistakes.

God doesn't condemn you.

You are precious and valuable in his eyes. He has plans for you – plans that are amazing. Keep your focus on him and you'll come through this stronger, more compassionate, more loving and more lovable. You will glorify him as a healed individual in ways you never could before this happened.

Take God at his word to love and comfort you. Let him surround you like the warmth of the sun, bringing you out of the darkness and into the light.

For you were once darkness, but now you are light in the Lord.
Live as children of light (for the fruit of the
light consists in all goodness, righteousness and
truth) and find out what pleases the Lord.
Ephesians 5:8-10 (NIV)

Blessings in your journey.
Lynn

DAY ONE
GOD CARES

The Lord is a refuge for the oppressed, a
stronghold in times of trouble.
Those who know your name will trust in you;
for you, Lord, have never forsaken those who seek you.
~Psalm 9:9-10 (NIV)

When you are in the depths of pain, you can feel like a small boat adrift in a sea of despair. As if everyone has abandoned, forgotten or turned against you, .

Your heart aches for a secure harbor where you can regroup and renew your strength.

God is the port you're looking for. He is your shelter from the world, a safe place for you in difficult times. He knows the challenges you're facing and he offers a respite from the madness.

This stronghold is available to you just by seeking him. Plugging in daily to the power source - God's word - and recharging your spiritual battery gives you the energy you need to get through your day of work, children, friendships, duties, bills and adversity.

Begin by trusting God. Believe he is with you, by your side every step. Know that you can lean on him. He has never forsaken anyone who has sought him out.

The Message Bible (TMB) restates the same verse this way:

God's a safe-house for the battered, a sanctuary during bad times. The moment you arrive, you relax; you're never sorry you knocked.

Today's assignment is to take him up on his word. Make God your stronghold in troubled times Find sanctuary in him and let yourself rest on his promises.

DAY TWO
GOD CAN HANDLE IT

God is a safe place to hide, ready to help when we need him.
We stand fearless at the cliff-edge of doom,
courageous in sea-storm and earthquake,
Before the rush and roar of oceans,
the tremors that shift mountains.
Jacob-wrestling God fights for us, God-
of-Angel-Armies protects us.
~Psalm 46:1-3 (TMB)

When bad things happen, sometimes all you want to do is hide. It's tempting to turn to escape avenues that aren't healthy, such as sex, drugs or alcohol. The problem is these are not safe havens. Even less harmful pursuits can serve as temporary fixes, but that doesn't make them a good choice. We saw yesterday how God is a sanctuary, and here's another verse that reminds us that God is a safe place.

He is powerful. A friend of mine was recently caught in a series of tornados and floods. As she left the area, the airplane rose to a elevation above the devastation and she could look down on the turbulence of the funnels, clouds and lightning. It was a spectacular view and one that affirmed for her that God is bigger than tornados.

He makes us fearless before the storms of life.

Today I'd like you to think about and write down a time when God was a safe haven for you. How did that feel?

DAY THREE
WHEN IT SEEMS LIKE ALL IS AGAINST YOU

Count on it: Everyone who had it in for you
will end up out in the cold- real losers.
Those who worked against you will end up empty-handed-
nothing to show for their lives.

When you go out looking for your old
adversaries you won't find them-
Not a trace of your old enemies, not even a memory.
That's right. Because I, your God, have a firm
grip on you and I'm not letting go.
I'm telling you, "Don't panic. I'm right here to help you."
~Isaiah 41:11-13 (TMB)

When you are going through rough times, it can feel like no one is on your side. A divorce robs you of your spouse and can cost you friends. Your family sometimes withdraws or can't cope. You're scared and alone.

People can be mean and hurtful. You wonder how life can be so unfair and inequitable. How can wickedness thrive while you suffer?

You might be tempted to try to even the score yourself, thinking no one else will. But don't be fooled. Evil will be punished, but God will be the one making the judgments. It's not your job and you don't have to spend time getting revenge.

You have more important things to do.

You are in the firm grip of God and his justice is perfect, even if you aren't able to see how it all unfolds.

The New International Version (NIV) says the same verse like this:

All who rage against you will surely be ashamed and disgraced; those who oppose you will be as nothing and perish. Though you search for your enemies, you will not find them. Those who wage war against you will be as nothing at all. For I am the LORD, your God, who takes hold of your right hand and says to you, Do not fear; I will help you.

He can vanquish your enemies and those who wage war, but it will be in his time and place. We don't have to worry about justice because he is in charge of it all. Today's assignment is to take a situation, big or small, where your instinct is to seek revenge but you are willing to lay it at God's feet and let him handle it.

Then let it go.

DAY FOUR
FEAR NOT

So we say with confidence,
"The Lord is my helper; I will not be afraid.
What can man do to me?"
~Hebrews 13:6 (NIV)

Sometimes it feels like "man" can do a lot, and it seems there are many things to fear. You might be afraid you won't have a place to live, or money to pay the bills, or that your car might fall apart, or that you will never be loved again.

These fears might be rational. Or they might be like a panic attack - feeling real but with no basis in fact.

Either way, if you make room for them in your life fears are delighted to move in and take over. They will dictate your decisions, taint your relationships and hamstring your progress.

When you feel fear, you can be confident it's not from God. In fact, one of the most frequent commands in the Bible is to "fear not". Our Creator knows how destructive fear can be, and he has the antidote.

He IS the antidote.

God is calling us to reject fear and find courage. The dictionary defines courage this way:

- the ability to do something that frightens one: she called on all her courage to face the ordeal,
- strength in the face of pain or grief: he fought his illness with great courage.

You have God's help, encouragement and support to do this. Banish fear and live boldly, secure in the knowledge that this is part of God's plan for you.

Write down one fear you will replace with trust.

DAY FIVE
REST ASSURED

You can go to bed without fear;
you will lie down and sleep soundly.
You need not be afraid of sudden disaster
or the destruction that comes upon the wicked,
for the Lord is your security. He will keep
your foot from being caught in a trap.
Proverbs 3:24-26 (NLT)

With so much going wrong in the world, and turbulence in your own life, a good night's sleep can be elusive. The act of laying down on your bed can unleash a string of thoughts you may have been able to hold at bay during the busy day.

Scenarios of disaster or destruction unfold like a 3D movie, and instead of relaxing, you become tense and wide awake.

You'd give a lot for a sound sleep, free of fears. Proverbs 3 tells us that wisdom will ease our sleep, and we can gain wisdom by keeping the teachings and commandments of the Lord. This chapter is full of great advice and precious guidance.

Today I'd like you to read Proverbs 3, pick one thing you intend to practice and write down how you will do that.

DAY SIX
MANAGING YOUR THOUGHTS

Those who are dominated by the sinful nature think about sinful things, but those who are controlled by the Holy Spirit think about things that please the Spirit. So letting your sinful nature control your mind leads to death. But letting the Spirit control your mind leads to life and peace.
Romans 8:5-6 (NLT)

When you're going through difficult times, it's hard to control your thoughts. You might be thinking of revenge, worried about your future, fearing a decision by a judge, letting hate simmer like an evil stew.

Your thoughts plague you. You might feel like you can't control them. But you can. Not instantly, and maybe not without some serious practice, but you can control them.

I don't think the battle to control our thoughts is new. Paul wrote to the Philippians (4:8 NIV);

Finally, brothers, whatever is true, whatever is noble, whatever is right, whatever is pure, whatever is lovely, whatever is admirable—if anything is excellent or praiseworthy—think about such things.

One proven technique to manage your thoughts is to replace them with something positive. If you watch or read too much news, you know how it can drag you down. Imagine spending the bulk of your days thinking about things that are true, excellent and lovely.

Your challenge today is to write down at least three things that are true, excellent and lovely, then shift your focus to them when your mind begins to dwell on unwanted thoughts.

DAY SEVEN
GRATITUDE LISTS

Always giving thanks to God the Father for everything,
in the name of our Lord Jesus Christ.
Ephesians 5:8 (NIV)

One thing that will help you in controlling your thoughts and bring you more happiness is to keep a gratitude list. Researchers have found people who consider things daily for which they are grateful are happier, healthier and have better relationships.

The studies had people list five things they were grateful for every night before they went to sleep and found that, within a short time, the participants reported greater well-being and a more positive outlook. The researchers only confirm what God teaches; that giving thanks is a constant act that benefits us and glorifies God.

It's similar to what we learned yesterday, confirming Paul's advice that it's best to dwell on that which is good and true. Happiness follows. And in case you wonder if God wants you to be happy, consider this:

Be joyful always; pray continually; give thanks in all circumstances, for this is God's will for you in Christ Jesus.
1 Thessalonians 5:16-18 (NIV)

Giving thanks even when life is a struggle is what God wants.

Being joyful and praying is what God wants. Researchers have now proven that what God wants for us improves our lives.

It should be no surprise.

Starting today and continuing through the next three weeks, make a list every night before you go to sleep of five things for which you are grateful.

DAY EIGHT

WORRY IS A WASTE OF TIME

Therefore do not worry about tomorrow, for tomorrow will worry about itself.
Each day has enough trouble of its own.
~Matthew 6:34 (NIV)

It's said that 90% of the things we spend time worrying about never happen. Yet it's where we often camp out, knee deep in fabricated fears and self-inflicted stress. Does all that worrying accomplish anything?

Worrying has been compared to sitting in a rocking chair; it gives you something to do but you never get anywhere.

It's a close cousin to fear, and it's one way people deal with their fears, as if worry can gnaw fear down to a manageable size. Unfortunately the only thing worry wears away is your health and well-being. The best advice I heard about worrying was; examine the situation or concern, determine if you can do something about, then do it. If you can't do anything about it, set it aside. Don't worry about what hasn't yet happened.

Another friend phrased it like this - *stay where your feet are.*

That's not to say you should stop being responsible. Don't run up a huge credit card bill and justify it by saying you simply don't worry about the future anymore. You shouldn't stop saving money, brushing your teeth or planting a garden, because these things will reap benefits later. The point is you shouldn't spend precious time fretting over what hasn't yet, or might never, happen.

I have this quote by Corrie ten Boom taped to my mirror. Corrie survived the holocaust and knew something about worry and fear of the future and she said this:

Worry does not empty tomorrow of its sorrow;
it empties today of its strength.

This quote touches my heart, especially coming from a woman who had so much personal devastation.

Jesus put it in perfect perspective when he asked if anyone can add one hour to his life by worrying. Well?

Of course no one can.

He goes on to say, if you can't add a single hour to your life by worrying, why do you bother worrying about anything? It's a plain fact you aren't going to be able to change it.

Today I'd like you to write down a worry that you have that has not happened and you know probably won't. Then feed it to the shredder or burn it in the fire pit, releasing it to God.

DAY NINE
WHAT TO DO INSTEAD OF WORRYING

Don't worry about anything; instead, pray about everything.
Tell God what you need, and thank him for all he has done.
Then you will experience God's peace, which
exceeds anything we can understand.
His peace will guard your hearts and
minds as you live in Christ Jesus.
Philippians 4:6-7 (NLT)

The thing about worry is it gives us something to do. Like a dog with a bone, we can work at it until our jaw aches. Unlike the dog and bone, we don't gradually make it smaller through our efforts. For us, it's more like a rock, breaking our teeth and refusing to yield.

If you quit worrying, what will you do instead? Fortunately we have good advice. Pray about everything. Talk to God about your needs, your concerns, your fears. Thank him for everything he's done, and recognize he has blessed you in the midst of this situation.

What will you get when you do this? The answer to all your prayers?

It doesn't say that. However, you will get peace. An amazing peace. A peace allows you to function at your best, knowing God has your back. He guards your heart and your mind as you go through your days.

Today I'd like you to take another worry and pray about it. Tell God everything, and thank him.

Let it go.

Then let his peace flow over you.

DAY TEN
TRUSTING GOD IS KEY

But blessed is the man who trusts in the
LORD, whose confidence is in him.
He will be like a tree planted by the water that
sends out its roots by the stream.
It does not fear when heat comes; its leaves are always green.
It has no worries in a year of drought
and never fails to bear fruit.
Jeremiah 17:7-8 (NIV)

It seems everything we use today has a battery, and a limited battery life. The computer I'm using right now is fully charged, but over the course of the day will run down until I need to recharge it.

I charge my cell phone every night, but occasionally I use it so much the battery gets low in the middle of the day. When that happens, if I haven't been paying attention to the signal, it quits on me. Goes dead. It's useless until I plug it in and get it recharged.

Trusting in God, putting your confidence in him, is like connecting to our power source. We never want to be too far from it, because with a steady supply of energy, we can flourish. In the tough times, if we are plugged in, we will survive. Not only survive, but be fruitful and productive.

The things we have discussed to this point are all ways you can invest your confidence in God. Spend time with him. Talk to him. Study his Word.

Today I'd like you to keep practicing the lessons we've learned so far, and don't forget your gratitude list.

DAY ELEVEN
GOD PROVIDES

Then, turning to his disciples, Jesus said,
"That is why I tell you not to worry about everyday life—
whether you have enough food to eat
or enough clothes to wear.
For life is more than food, and your body more than clothing.
Look at the ravens. They don't plant or harvest
or store food in barns, for God feeds them.
And you are far more valuable to him than any birds!"
Luke 12:22-24 (NLT)

We spend a lot of time fretting over whether we have enough. It's a hot button for me. For whatever reason, somewhere in my formative years I felt a fundamental lack and the seed of fear was planted. Would there be enough? What if it ran out before my turn? Would I be taken care of?

Jesus assures us that God provides. He cares for the smallest creatures in his world, and we are worth more to him than they are.

It's important to note that the birds don't simply sit on the ground, confident that God will give them everything. They forage for food, build nests, raise young – in other words, go about their lives. We need to go about our lives, too, but remember to keep God in the center of it all.

So do not worry, saying, 'What shall we eat?' or 'What shall we drink?' or 'What shall we wear?' For the pagans

run after all these things, and your heavenly Father knows that you need them. But seek first his kingdom and his righteousness, and all these things will be given to you as well.
Matthew 6: 31-33 (NIV)

Keep your priorities straight. Put God first and God will provide for you. He knows what you need.

Take a moment today to write about what worries you might have been putting ahead of God. Reorganize your priorities so that your first focus is on God and practice trusting him. Write about how this will look in your life.

DAY TWELVE

TRUE RECOVERY

Come to me, all you who are weary and
burdened, and I will give you rest.
Matthew 11:28 (NIV)

TMB says it this way:

Are you tired? Worn out? Burned out on religion?
Come to me. Get away with me and you'll recover
your life. I'll show you how to take a real rest.
Walk with me and work with me-watch how I
do it. Learn the unforced rhythms of grace.
I won't lay anything heavy or ill-fitting on you.
Keep company with me and you'll
learn to live freely and lightly.

If you seek complete recovery, know that it's possible with God. People can help, church can provide fellowship, recovery groups and coaching gives you a place to speak out and get guidance, but the true healing is within, a place that's only accessible to you and God.

His promise is like an oasis for your broken heart . . . your damaged ego . . . your hungry spirit. He is inviting you to bring it all to him. Trade it in for rest and peace. Not only that, but he will gently teach you what you need to know, being careful not to overload you or encumber you with something that's not right for you.

Wouldn't you like to learn the unforced rhythms of grace? It sounds lovely, doesn't it? Like an effortless dance of life in the arms of your Lord.

Would you like to live freely and lightly? With respite from your burdens? What a blessing that would be! And it's within your grasp. God doesn't promise to remove all difficulties, but he does offer to share them, easing the load.

Today let God take the weight off your shoulders. Walk with him, work with him to learn his ways. What's one thing God can teach you today?

DAY THIRTEEN
GRIEVING YOUR LOSS

For everything there is a season,
a time for every activity under heaven.
A time to be born and a time to die.
A time to plant and a time to harvest.
A time to kill and a time to heal.
A time to tear down and a time to build up.
A time to cry and a time to laugh.
A time to grieve and a time to dance.
Ecclesiastes 3:1-4 (NLT)

God provides powerful help, but maybe you still hurt. You might wonder why you are feeling such overwhelming heartache and misery from your divorce. Others have told you that divorce is common and you need to just get over it. And yet, the sorrow is in your bones, deep and painful.

Having faith in God doesn't mean you aren't going to experience human despair. He comes alongside to help you through it, but you still must acknowledge and respect the emotions you feel in order to be able to move past them.

No matter what your marriage was like, you once had hopes and dreams that it would be wonderful. You had visions of what your life would be like with that special person; perhaps raising children or growing old together. When the marriage died, the dream died. And the loss is as real as any literal death.

You are grieving.

You might tempted to try to dodge the pain or dismiss your feelings, thinking that by minimizing what you've lost you can box it up and stick it on a shelf where you can ignore it.

Remember the broken leg? You would be foolish to look at it and say "it's nothing, other people have gone through worse, I'm going to just go on with my life", then step out as if your leg was sound.

A wise person recognizes the reality of the broken leg, or broken heart, and responds accordingly. Your life has changed. There will be a time to move on, and a time to dance again, but right now it's okay for you to cry and grieve.

Your sadness is valid and normal. Give yourself permission to feel your feelings even if it's scary. Allow whatever time it takes to go through it. Be kind to yourself, as you would be to a friend.

Of course, if you find you are slipping into serious or clinical depression, don't hesitate to get professional help. God has much to offer us as we go through difficulties, and sometimes he offers it in the form of other people.

Give yourself a hug today and let you be you.

DAY FOURTEEN
GOD HEARS YOUR CALL

I love the Lord because he hears my voice and my prayer for mercy. Because he bends down to listen, I will pray as long as I have breath!
Psalm 116:1-2 (NLT)

Have you ever called a company for help and gotten trapped in voice-mail wasteland? Press this button for that, that button for this, all the while they assure you that they value your business. Sure they do. The feeling I get is that they value my money, but really don't want to have to talk to me.

Listening is not only polite, it's required if you are going to have a meaningful relationship. God wants a meaningful relationship with you. Not one where you get his pre-recorded message, but one where he leans down to catch the words you speak. What a picture that creates in my mind!

Loving parents, attentive and focused, bend toward their children to hear every word. It may be nonsense, but it's important to that parent.

The NIV says it this way; *He turned his ear to me, He heard my voice.*

We don't pray to a stone god, a picture or a plastic figure, we pray to a living God, who hears us. Who wants to have a relationship.

When you pray today, know that God is listening. Pour out your heart. He hears your cry, and you can call on him forever.

What do you want to say to him?

DAY FIFTEEN
GOD'S PEACE

I am leaving you with a gift—peace of mind and heart.
And the peace I give is a gift the world cannot give.
So don't be troubled or afraid.
John 14:27 (NLT)

Everyone likes gifts. The promise, in the shiny box or pretty paper, of your heart's desire. The anticipation of revealing the treasure inside. Our gifts to each other are usually material things, some longed for, others practical or necessary. Some gifts are a combination of both.

The gift of peace is an amazing thing. The dictionary defines peace as;

- freedom from disturbance
- serenity
- mental calm

People search the world for peace of mind and heart, yet it's not in any location or building or physical pose, it's in you, a gift that Jesus, speaking for God, has left for us.

You will keep in perfect peace all who trust in you,
all whose thoughts are fixed on you!
Trust in the Lord always,
for the Lord God is the eternal Rock.
Isaiah 26:3-4

Perfect peace can be yours. Peace of mind and heart. It's a gift. For you. Unwrap it today and hold it close. How will your life change when you have peace of mind and heart?

DAY SIXTEEN
QUIET TIME

Be still, and know that I am God;
I will be exalted among the nations,
I will be exalted in the earth.
Psalm 46:10 (NIV)

Being still is not one of my talents. While I acknowledge that multitasking is just a myth I'm not willing to give up on it quite yet. My days are full and my schedule is planned weeks in advance. Busy is my middle name.

Without a burning bush or pillar, how will I hear God? I won't, unless I take the time to be still and know he is God. Unless I quiet my hectic day and listen.

Prayer time is also meditation time. The word meditation has become entwined with a specific mind set that carries a negative connotation for many Christians. Yet the word meditation means:

- to focus one's mind for a period of time
- to think deeply or carefully about (something)

How you focus or think deeply and carefully can vary. Certain verses in the Bible suggest we meditate on the law day and night. I usually read a passage and consider a specific scripture. The important thing is to be still at some point and listen for God.

May my meditation be pleasing to him,
as I rejoice in the LORD.
Psalm 104:34

Rejoice in God and let your thoughts, your focus, your meditation be pleasing to him today. What verse or thought about God can you focus on or think deeply about in the next 24 hours?

DAY SEVENTEEN
YOUR REFUGE

I run for dear life to God, I'll never live to regret it.
Do what you do so well:
get me out of this mess and up on my feet.
Put your ear to the ground and listen,
give me space for salvation.
Be a guest room where I can retreat;
you said your door was always open!
You're my salvation—my vast, granite fortress.
Psalm 71:1-3 (TMB)

We've already talked about how God is our refuge and how he gives us the strength we need to live our lives. But it bears repeating.

Sometimes when we are into the Word and trying to get close to God, obstacles will arise to distract and discourage us. You might have had some things come up in the past few weeks that are especially challenging and you might be wondering how you are going to handle everything going on in your life.

It's a good time to remember who God is and how he is here for us. He can get us on our feet when we have no hope and can't form a plan. He gives us space and is always available.

You can run to God, he is waiting with open arms. He delights in being there for you and being your rock of refuge. He wants to rescue and deliver you from worldly predicaments.

What might be plaguing you? What are you finding unbearable? Write it down, then make it a point to turn to him before you consider any other option.

You'll never regret it.

DAY EIGHTEEN
FAITH IS A SOLID FOUNDATION

The fundamental fact of existence is that
this trust in God, this faith,
is the firm foundation under everything
that makes life worth living.
It's our handle on what we can't see.
The act of faith is what distinguished our
ancestors, set them above the crowd.
Hebrews 11:1-2 (TMB)

In the beginning of this series, I talked about building a framework of support to help you heal and recover from life's setbacks. Here you see that faith, trusting God, is the foundation upon which everything else stands.

A strong foundation is crucial to the stability and durability of a structure, and the foundation of your life should not be on shifting sands like money, other people, jobs or status.

I went through a period in my life where everything I had thought defined me crumbled. I lost my standing, my finances, my friends, my identity. Nothing remained except me, and I wasn't feeling too worthwhile. I was down to bare metal and had to figure out who I was and what life I intended to live.

It was, to say the least, humbling.

But priceless.

Because when you lose everything you once took for granted you have the unique opportunity to begin again, rebuilding a life that reflects who you really are. Rebuilding on a firm foundation.

Faith.

A life built on faith in God is truly a life worth living. And it's yours for the taking.

There are very few things that are unshakable. None that I can think of, except for God. I don't want to spend time investing in something that could be here today and gone tomorrow. What about you?

Today take a moment to examine your foundation. Does it set you above the crowd?

DAY NINETEEN
DEEP ROOTS EQUAL STRONG TREES

Then Christ will make his home in your
hearts as you trust in him.
Your roots will grow down into God's love and keep you strong.
And may you have the power to understand,
as all God's people should,
how wide, how long, how high, and how deep his love is.
May you experience the love of Christ, though
it is too great to understand fully.
Then you will be made complete with all the fullness
of life and power that comes from God.
Ephesians 3:17-19 (NLT)

Another way to look at your foundation is to consider the roots of a tree. We look at trees from the ground up and admire their foliage and branches. But the real action is beneath our feet. Trees gain nourishment from their roots. Trees with strong roots are healthy trees.

When you make room in your heart for Jesus, he fills the empty space. It takes trust to make room. It takes leaning on him in tough times and giving thanks in all times.

The dictionary says trust means;

- to be sure of
- to commit to
- to count on

When you count on God, his presence grows. Your roots dig into him for stability and strength. You begin to get a glimpse of how immense his love is and your life expands.

No person can meet that need like God can. If you look for another romantic relationship before you develop your relationship with God, you're not going to get the satisfaction in your life you seek.

God makes your life complete. Seek him first and he will bring you what you long for.

Delight yourself in the LORD and he will
give you the desires of your heart.
Psalm 37:4 (NIV)

Write down what some of the desires of your heart. Not your wish list, not your material desires, but the true desires of your heart.

DAY TWENTY
MORE THAN JUST WORDS

But don't just listen to God's word. You must do what it says.
Otherwise, you are only fooling yourselves.
For if you listen to the word and don't obey, it
is like glancing at your face in a mirror.
You see yourself, walk away, and forget what you look like.
But if you look carefully into the perfect
law that sets you free, and
if you do what it says and don't forget what you heard,
then God will bless you for doing it.
James 1:22-25 (NLT)

When my children were growing up there were times they grew weary of my parental guidance. I remember one instance when they were young and we had the discussion that goes on in every household.

Clean your room, I'd say. *Okay*, came the reply. An hour later I'd go check on things to find them playing with toys. *Clean your room now!* I'd repeat. *OKAY!* They'd say again.

An hour later, same thing. No change.

They heard me. They agreed with me. But they did nothing about it and the room remained a mess.

It's the same for us. It's not enough to read the Bible. It's not enough to be able to quote scripture. God knows the difference

between lip service and true obedience.
He knows the intent of your heart.

When you study God's word, you want it to stick. You want to put it into action.

TMB puts it like this:

Don't fool yourself into thinking that you are a listener when you are anything but, letting the Word go in one ear and out the other. Act on what you hear! Those who hear and don't act are like those who glance in the mirror, walk away, and two minutes later have no idea who they are, what they look like. But whoever catches a glimpse of the revealed counsel of God—the free life!—even out of the corner of his eye, and sticks with it, is no distracted scatterbrain but a man or woman of action. That person will find delight and affirmation in the action.

Review the truths you've learned the past three weeks and select a few (for starters) that you will act on today, this week and this year.

DAY TWENTY-ONE
FORGIVENESS IS POWERFUL

Bear with each other and forgive whatever grievances you may have against one another. Forgive as the Lord forgave you.
Colossians 3:13 (NIV)

Forgiveness is not optional. God expects us to forgive. He also knows how difficult it can be.

You've been wronged. It's human nature to harbor resentment and anger toward the person who treated you badly. It's human nature, but God wants us to strive for more than mere human response.

Forgiveness is possible because we are forgiven. Because Jesus died on the cross for our sins, the sacrifice was made and we were forgiven. He died in our place, yet all we have to do is to believe and accept him as our savior. We don't have to do penance or give any sacrifice of our own. We don't need to earn our salvation. It's by the grace of God, a pure gift. We only have to accept it.

For God loved the world so much that he gave his one and only Son, so that everyone who believes in him will not perish but have eternal life.
John 3:16 (NLT)

We've all done wrong. No matter how hard you struggle to live a good life, be a good person, sometime, someplace you're going to mess up. Maybe you've messed up in big ways. If we had to pay for every infraction, we'd have a debt it would take several lifetimes to eliminate. But Jesus died and wiped it out. Forgave it. Freed us.

One thing he asks is for us to forgive others. In case you wonder how much we should forgive, he says; *Forgive as we are forgiven.*

Maybe you just can't imagine it. Maybe your pain is so deep, your hurt so scarring that you don't think forgiveness is possible.

If you're not ready to make the decision to forgive - and forgiveness is a decision, not a feeling - begin by asking God to give you the desire to forgive and work your way towards it. God recognizes your willingness to consider it and sees you are taking steps to get there. He'll help you.

Who in your life does God wants you to forgive? Do you feel far from that step?

Begin by writing your intention. Then ask God for His power and strength.

DAY TWENTY-TWO
LOVING OTHERS

Do not seek revenge or bear a grudge
against one of your people,
but love your neighbor as yourself. I am the LORD.
Leviticus 19:18 (NIV)

Some people are easy to love. My children. My grandchildren. My sons-in-law and their families.

Others are almost impossible.

We've been taught that it's wrong to love yourself, but if you're not supposed to love yourself, how would this verse make any sense? God knows we love ourselves, we take care of ourselves and we maintain ourselves. What he's saying is he wants us to bring that same level of care to others. He wants us to consider their needs and their circumstances the same way we consider our own.

He also warns against holding grudges or seeking revenge. This is so much harder to do than it sounds. It's my opinion that of all the things God asks of us, this is one of the most difficult. It offends our sensibilities to be told we must love everyone, even our enemies.

I'm also convinced that's exactly why it's so important to him. What better measure of faith and trust than loving those who you don't even like?

Loving isn’t the same as trusting and you can love without taking foolish chances. God wants you to love others, he doesn't say that they will be kind and loving toward you.

Love with intention, without expectation.

If you do, in true God fashion, blessings will follow.

You've heard stories of people whose lives have been radically changed by love. People who never felt valued discover they are loved and it turns their world on its head. Imagine, if everyone consciously practiced loving one another, how different things would be?

Who comes to mind? Throw love at them like rose petals. See what happens.

DAY TWENTY-THREE
REACH OUT

Therefore encourage one another and build each other up, just as in fact you are doing.
1 Thessalonians 5:11 (NIV)

Encouragement is important, especially when people are struggling. When Paul wrote this letter to the Thessalonians, they were facing some of the same challenges Christians are today. There was dissension between believers and difficulties with non-believers. Paul wanted to recognize the value of their support and encouragement for each other.

For the past three-plus weeks, you've been leaning into God, relying on His promises and strength. Now it's time to exercise and test the new strength you've gained.

Keep your eyes open for someone around you whom you can love and fortify. Is there someone you can build up, in an honest and authentic way? Is there a friend who needs an encouraging word? Positive feedback?

Is there someone who has done much for you, but you forgot to thank?

Do it now.

When you are going through divorce or other trying times, you tend to meet others battling similar situations or life-challenges. When you do, take the opportunity to minister to them and yourself at the same time. That's right. Supporting others reflects back into your own life and gives you a lift, too.

By taking even tiny steps to reach out you are moving toward healing and recovery. It's like physical therapy for that broken leg. It's part of the overall process.

Write down names of those whom you can love and support. Someone who's facing their own challenges and could use a kind word. Then take action.

DAY TWENTY-FOUR
CONTINUING EDUCATION

These are the proverbs of Solomon, David's son, king of Israel.
Their purpose is to teach people wisdom and discipline,
to help them understand the insights of the wise.

Their purpose is to teach people to live
disciplined and successful lives,
to help them do what is right, just, and fair.

These proverbs will give insight to the simple,
knowledge and discernment to the young.
Proverbs 1:1-4 (NLT)

Most professions require continuing education credits. It's a way to ensure the person is well-educated in their field and has thorough knowledge. We need continued education, too. We need to keep inputting vital information.

The Bible is our textbook, God's guidelines for living.

Reading it not only brings us closer to God, we gain practical instruction on what our lives should look like.

In Proverbs 2 it says to seek wisdom, search for it like you would for precious gems. Wisdom will enter your heart and knowledge will fill you with joy. Your choices and understanding will keep you safe. Proverbs 3 tells you that if you trust in the Lord and seek his will in what you do, he'll show you what path to take.

You can see how important this continuing education is to your life.

We are four days from the completion of this series. This is a good time to make a plan to continue your education so you won't be left high and dry when you finish this book. Proverbs is a good place to begin.

Today, create a reading schedule that you can start as soon as Comfort Verses ends. As you read, plan to ask yourself questions about what you've read so you get the most from it.

CHAPTER TWENTY-FIVE
GOD KNOWS YOU AND LOVES YOU

You made all the delicate, inner parts of my body
and knit me together in my mother's womb.
Thank you for making me so wonderfully complex!
Your workmanship is marvelous—how well I know it.
You watched me as I was being formed in utter seclusion,
as I was woven together in the dark of the womb.
You saw me before I was born.
Every day of my life was recorded in your book.
Every moment was laid out before a single day had passed.
Psalm 139:13-16

If anyone really knew me, they wouldn't like me.

If you've ever had this thought, guess what?

You're human.

We present our best face to the world, but it doesn't always tell the whole story. And that's appropriate in certain situations.

I don't know about you, but if I get a brand-new doctor when I go to the emergency room, I don't want him telling me he's scared, or that he's never done this before or he isn't sure how to diagnose my ills.

I want confidence.

If I listen to a keynote speaker, I don't want apologies because his power-point didn't load, or he lost his notes, or he has a case of nerves because it's the first time he's spoken in front of such a large group. If he wants my attention for the next hour, at least ACT like a professional.

Yes, there are times to fake it and let your abilities catch up, because people do judge you by how you present yourself.

But God doesn't.

God knows you inside and out. He knows every secret, every hidden thought and desire. When you come before him, you don't need to fake righteousness, you don't need to pretend. You can be who you are, mistakes and all, laying it out with complete transparency. He knows. He knew the instant it happened. Don't try to impress God, just be who you are.

Confess everything and don't hold back. He forgives, and only asks that you are truly sorry and will change.

What if you're not completely sorry? What if you were mean to someone and still feel like they deserved it?

God knows. He *knows*! So be honest with him - confess that you don't feel remorse, even though you were in the wrong. Ask him to work in your heart so you'll let go of the resentment that's making you act mean or hateful. Ask him to change your feelings. Then let him. Stop resisting forgiveness. Quit hoarding your anger, stoking it with resentful thoughts, collecting situations that fortify your wall of resentment.

I promise you, as long as you look for things to “justify”

your bad feelings, you will find them. So stop looking! Let the hurtful things that happen pass you by. Don't grab them, saying "See? I told you so!" to anyone who listens.

Be honest with God. Identify the problem areas. Give them to him and live in faith and trust.

He knows everything about you and loves you regardless! He sees the person you are now and the person you can become and he loves you.

Today, when you come before God, tell him how you really feel. Don't hold back. Then ask for His help and surrender. Write those things down you are giving to him, then burn, shred or otherwise destroy them. It's between you and God.

CHAPTER TWENTY-SIX
HOPE AND A FUTURE

For I know the plans I have for you," says the Lord.
"They are plans for good and not for disaster,
to give you a future and a hope."
Jeremiah 29:11 (NLT)

After my divorce I felt hopeless. I'd always been a planner, a goal-setter, an achiever. It had defined me. Divorce happened and I found I had no vision and couldn't form a plan. I felt like I'd lost a significant part of my identity at a time when I'd already taken a body blow in that department.

Being unable to picture a future left me scared and uncertain, hopeless and depressed. When I read this verse it gave me such comfort. Even though *I* couldn't see a future, God could. He had a plan for me, one designed to help me thrive and prosper. He has a plan for you, too.

God's intention is for us to be the best we can be, serving him, trusting him and moving forward. He is our hope and he guides us through the times when we can't see the path.

"But I'll take the hand of those who don't know
the way, who can't see where they're going.
I'll be a personal guide to them, directing
them through unknown country.
I'll be right there to show them what roads to take,
make sure they don't fall into the ditch.
These are the things I'll be doing for them— sticking

with them, not leaving them for a minute."
Isaiah 42:16 (TMB)

When you talk to God today, ask him about the plans he has for you. Write down some of the things that come into your mind.

CHAPTER TWENTY-SEVEN
GOD'S GRACE IS OUR FREEDOM

For the grace of God has been revealed,
bringing salvation to all people.
And we are instructed to turn from godless
living and sinful pleasures.
We should live in this evil world with
wisdom, righteousness, and
devotion to God, while we look forward with hope to
that wonderful day when the glory of our great
God and Savior, Jesus Christ, will be revealed.
He gave his life to free us from every kind of sin, to cleanse us,
and to make us his very own people,
totally committed to doing good deeds.
Titus 2:11-13 (NLT)

Why aren't we in charge of our own salvation?

Some people think we should get to heaven by being a good person. How good would you have to be to earn heaven? Who would set the standard?

What about a person who gives money to feed the hungry and shelter the poor but abuses his child? Is that a good person? How about someone who is fun to be with and nice to everyone, but submits a false insurance claim?

Okay, false insurance claim, you say you might be able to excuse that... What about the Bernie Madoffs? What if Bernie had given 90% of his stolen loot to charity? Would that make him good? Good enough to get to heaven?

The problem is there are too many variables in human calculations. And things change. If people were in charge, would it be like taxes? Looking for loopholes? Unsure of the requirements?

What if you were given the keys to heaven but you had to give away all your money? Or sacrifice your livelihood? Or your children?

What is the cost of eternal life in the hereafter?

Priceless.

You could never pay enough. You don't have enough resources, enough valuable things. It's out of your reach.

But what if it was a gift?

There it is, sitting on the table. It's got your name on it. If you claim it, it's yours. If you don't, you'll never know.

If you have claimed God's gift of eternal life you already know that although it's based on grace, it changes you. You can't accept Jesus into your heart without a transformation in your behavior and your attitude. God wants you to live with wisdom, righteousness and devotion. Not as the world does, with greed and self-interest, but with love and compassion toward others.

You can do this because, as a child of God, you are clean. Past sins, no matter how bad, are gone.

You are not your sins, *you are not divorce,* you are not your mistakes.

You are one of God's people, committed to him and doing good deeds because it's who you are.

You are an important part of his Kingdom, no matter what has happened in your life.

It's quite a gift.

Make sure you don't leave it on the table.

CHAPTER TWENTY-EIGHT
COMFORT ENOUGH TO SHARE

All praise to God, the Father of our Lord Jesus Christ.
God is our merciful Father and the source of all comfort.
He comforts us in all our troubles so
that we can comfort others.
When they are troubled, we will be able to give them
the same comfort God has given us
2 Corinthians 1:3-4 (NLT)

We're at the end of the four-week series of comfort verses. I hope you've found comfort, peace and even some challenges along the way. I chose to end with this verse because it reminds me how God is our Father and the source of all our comfort.

I also like the idea of God comforting us so we can turn around and extend that same comfort to others. It's what inspired me to tell my story and coach others who face loss, life-crisis and major changes. And it falls right in line with God's commandment to love and care for each other.

"I have loved you even as the Father has loved me.
Remain in my love. When you obey my commandments,
you remain in my love, just as I obey my Father's
commandments and remain in his love. I have told
you these things so that you will be filled with my joy.
Yes, your joy will overflow! This is my commandment:
Love each other in the same way I have loved you."
John 15:9-12 (NLT)

Even though I may not know you, I picture you in my mind as I write. Even though our circumstances may be different, I have compassion for your pain. I've known pain, and I understand.

As I mentioned earlier, I lost all hope for a while and with God's help I've come back to a place that is better than anywhere else I've been. My life today is not perfect, not without troubles, but I've learned to be joyful and give thanks, trust God and live fully.

Obeying His commandments is not easy, and I'm not perfect. However I've seen the effects of committing to His word in my life and the lives of those around me, and I know it's not a casual request from God. It's important and our obedience allows him to accomplish things that are magnificent.

I hope these 28 days have given you assurance that you are not alone, you are loved and God has a plan to bless you no matter how old you are or in what circumstances you find yourself.

You can rebuild a life that's the best you've ever had. His Word gives you the tools you need to do that.

Now it's up to you.

AFTERWORD

Perhaps you've been reading this, not sure if you have accepted Jesus as your personal Savior. If you want the life discussed in these verses, you only need to do three things:

ADMIT that you need God, you've made mistakes (or sinned) and ask him to forgive your sins.

If we confess our sins to him, he is faithful and
just to forgive us and to cleanse us from every wrong.
1 John 1:9 (NLT)

BELIEVE Jesus died to pay the price for your sins and that he rose from the dead and is alive today. He is the only way to salvation.

If you confess with your mouth, 'Jesus is Lord,' and
believe in your heart that God
raised him from the dead,
you will be saved.
Romans 10:9 (NIV)

Salvation is found in no one else [Jesus],
for there is no other name by which we must be saved.
Acts 4:12, (NIV)

Jesus is the only One who can save people.
His name is the only power in the world
that has been given to save people.
We must be saved through him.

Acts 4:12 (New Century Version)

ACCEPT God's gift to you and start your new life fresh, clean and renewed. Let him transform you.

For it is by grace you have been saved, through faith—
and this is not from yourselves, it is the gift of God—
not by works, so that no one can boast.
Ephesians 2:8, 9 (NIV)

To all who received him, he gave the right to
become children of God.
All they needed to do was to
trust him to save them.
All those who believe this are reborn!—
not a physical rebirth...
but from the will of God.
John 1:12,13 (The Living Bible)

You can pray a simple prayer, such as:

I know I'm a sinner. I believe Jesus, Son of the living God, died for my sins when he died on the cross. I accept God's gift of salvation. I want him to be the Lord of my life.

Amen.

If you pray this prayer and want to tell me about it, I'd love to hear.

If my book, *Divorce is not Destiny* or *Comfort Verses for the Divorced Christian* helped or encouraged you, please consider telling a few friends about it.

You can visit my website: DivorceisnotDestiny.com or contact me at Lynn@DivorceisnotDestiny.com

Blessings and joy to you.

Lynn

www.ingramcontent.com/pod-product-compliance
Lightning Source LLC
LaVergne TN
LVHW010617100826
845148LV00014B/3002

* 9 7 8 0 9 8 2 6 7 7 1 0 0 *